W9-BUZ-816

PRESERVING BASICS

A FIREFLY BOOK

Published by Firefly Books Ltd. 2011

Copyright © 2011 Marabout

All rights reserved. No part of this publication may be reproduced, stored in a retrieval system, or transmitted in any form or by any means, electronic, mechanical, photocopying, recording or otherwise, without the prior written permission of the Publisher.

First printing

Publisher Cataloging-in-Publication Data (U.S.)
Vassallo, Jody.
   Preserving basics / 77 recipes illustrated step by step / Jody Vassallo ; photography by Clive Bozzard-Hill.
[256] p. : col. photos. ; cm. (My Cooking Class)
Includes index.
Summary: A photographic, step-by-step guide to making jellies, jam, chutneys, mustards, spreads, marmalades and relishes.
ISBN-13: 978-1-55407-942-1 (pbk.)
1. Condiments. I. Bozzard-Hill, Clive. II. Title. III. Series.
641.814 dc22   TX819.A1V3883 2011

Library and Archives Canada Cataloguing in Publication
Vassallo, Jody
   Preserving basics : 77 recipes illustrated step by step / Jody Vassallo ; photographs by Clive Bozzard-Hill.
(My cooking class)
Includes index.
Translation of: Les basiques confitures.
ISBN 978-1-55407-942-1
   1. Canning and preserving. 2. Cookbooks. I. Bozzard-Hill, Clive II. Title. III. Series: My cooking class
TX601.V3813 2011   641.4'2   C2011-901603-6

Published in the United States by
Firefly Books (U.S.) Inc.
P.O. Box 1338, Ellicott Station
Buffalo, New York 14205

Published in Canada by
Firefly Books Ltd.
66 Leek Crescent
Richmond Hill, Ontario L4B 1H1

Printed in Canada

MY COOKING CLASS

PRESERVING BASICS

77 RECIPES
ILLUSTRATED STEP BY STEP

JODY VASSALLO

PHOTOGRAPHY BY CLIVE BOZZARD-HILL

* * *

FIREFLY BOOKS

BASICS

INTRODUCTION

Preserving fruits and vegetables in the form of jam and other preserves, such as jellies, curds and chutneys, can be one of the most rewarding and relaxing things you do in your kitchen. There is nothing more satisfying than cooking up a big pot of jam and sharing the fruits of your labor — in jars — with your friends. Equally enjoyable is sitting down to breakfast and opening a jar of your latest jam or serving a plate of cheese with some homemade quince cheese and a selection of mouthwatering chutneys.

Jams are made by boiling fruit and sugar together until they reach a setting point. A jelly is made using strained fruit juice, which is then boiled with sugar to form a clear jelled liquid. Marmalades are similar to jams but are made with citrus fruit. Curds are custard-like mixtures made from fruit juice or puree that has been cooked with eggs, sugar and butter. Fruit butters and cheeses have a firm texture and are made by boiling cooked pureed fruit and sugar together, then either set jarred or into molds or cut into pieces and coated in sugar. A mustard is a condiment made from the seeds (yellow or black) of the mustard plant and blended with water and other flavorings, such as wine, vinegar and herbs. A chutney is made by cooking fruit and/or vegetables with sugar, vinegar and spices to form a reduced thick, concentrated pulp. These are best left to mature for several weeks before using.

The secret to a successful jam or chutney is in the equipment you use, the quality of ingredients and how organized you are.

✳ ✳ ✳

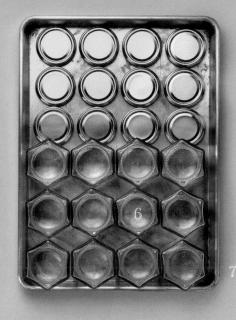

EQUIPMENT

❖ THERE ARE A FEW PIECES OF EQUIPMENT THAT YOU WILL NEED TO MAKE LIFE A BIT EASIER ❖

1. Preserving pan/stockpot/boiling water canner: A heavy pan is essential. This allows you to sterilize jars and rapidly boil sugared fruit without it sticking to the bottom. Boiling water canners are a handy tool, as they often have a metal insert into which you can slot your filled jars. **2. Ladle:** A ladle that fits into the mouth of jams jars is useful when filling jars. **3. Skimming spoon:** Useful for removing any scum from the surface of jams. **4. Long-handled wooden spoon:** Essential when making jams. To clean, soak in lemon juice and water and dry in a low oven.

5. Tongs: To remove cheesecloth bags or spice baskets. **6. Jars:** Jars should have proper vacuum-seal lids (not pictured) with removable screw-top bands (not pictured). Bands can be reused, but you should always use new seals. Jars should be sterilized in boiling water and left to air dry. **7. Metallic baking dishes:** Used to warm sugar on. **8. Chopping board and fruit knife:** Used to cut up fruits and vegetables. **9. Thermometer:** Used to judge the setting point. One that clips onto the side of the pan is useful. Alternatively, use the wrinkle test (see step 8 on the following page).

10. Jam funnel: This is used to help fill jars. **11. Tea towel:** Useful for holding jars when filling them. **12. Pastry brush:** Used to brush down the sides of the pan with a little water at the start, as undissolved sugar can stick to the sides of the pan as you stir. **13. Measuring cups:** These are very handy for measuring your ingredients. **14. Heatproof jugs:** Used for filling jars. **15. Bowls:** Two large non-metallic bowls are invaluable. You will need these to soak fruit and drain fruit juice when making jelly. **16. Jelly bag and stand:** Invaluable when making jelly. Wash the bags and dry thoroughly immediately after using, then reuse them again and again. **17. Cheesecloth and string:** Used to enclose pits, stones, cores or

spices. **18. Scissors:** Useful for cutting paper and string to required sizes and lengths. **19. Parchment paper:** Used to cover fruits left to stand overnight. **20. Grater, zester, microplane:** These utensils can be used to remove the zest from citrus fruit. **21. Apple corer:** This is very handy if you are making a recipe that uses a lot of apples or pears. **22. Cherry pitter:** This is useful if you are making a recipe that uses a lot of cherries or olives. **23. Scale:** Used to measure large quantities of fruits or vegetables. **24. Timer:** Keeps track of cooking times; essential if you have a few jams on the go at once.

1
4
2
5
3
6

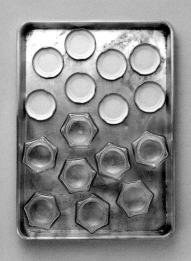

MAKING JAM

1	Wash jars, lids and bands in hot, soapy water. Then, rinse well and remove any old labels if you are reusing jars.	2	Preheat oven to 275°F (140°C). Put sugar on a baking sheet and warm in oven for 20 minutes. Put two small plates in the freezer.	3	Sterilize all jars, lids and bands in boiling water for at least 10 minutes.
4	Turn the jars right side up and leave to air dry.	5	Put fruit, sugar and lemon juice into a pan and stir gently until sugar dissolves, brushing down the sides with a wet pastry brush.	6	Boil, stirring a few times; use a large spoon to remove any scum from the surface and skim again, if necessary, before bottling.

7

8

9

10

11

12

7	Put a sugar thermometer into the pan while the jam is boiling. Most jams have a setting point of 220°F (105°C).	8	Alternatively, put a little jam on a frozen plate and freeze for 2 minutes. Push your finger through the jam, if the surface wrinkles, it is ready. If not, cook a little longer.	9	Ladle the jam into a heatproof jug — this will make filling the jars much easier.
10	Fill the jars to 1/8 inch (3mm) from the rim with the hot jam.	11	Experts used to recommend turning jars upside down to sterilize the lids. This is now considered unsafe. Instead, process in a boiling water canner.	12	Label, date and store (see storage chart in Appendix).

JAMS & ACCOMPANIMENTS

1

PEAR, GINGER & SPICE JAM

❖ MAKES 4 JARS (1 CUP/250 ML EACH) • PREPARATION: 20 MINUTES • COOKING: 1½ HOURS ❖

2 pounds (1 kg) firm, slightly under ripe pears
1 vanilla bean, cut in half lengthwise
6 slices fresh ginger
¼ teaspoon (1 ml) ground cinnamon
¼ teaspoon (1 ml) ground cloves

3¾ cups (925 ml) granulated sugar, warmed
2 tablespoons (30 ml) lemon juice
4 teaspoons (20 ml) butter

1

1 2
3 4

1	Peel and core the pears, reserving the cores and seeds. Roughly chop the pears. Put the cores and seeds into a cheesecloth bag and tie with string.	2	Put the pears into a large pan, add the vanilla bean halves, ginger, spices, cheesecloth bag and 4 cups (1 L) of water.	
3	Bring to a boil, then reduce the heat and simmer for 50 minutes, until the fruit is soft.	4	Add the sugar, lemon juice and butter and stir over low heat until the sugar has dissolved.	➢

5. Remove and discard the vanilla, ginger slices and cheesecloth bag. Return to a boil and cook, without stirring, for 20 minutes, until the jam reaches setting point. Remove from the heat and stir to remove the scum.

VARIATION

※

You can vary the spices you use in this jam — try cardamom, saffron, bay leaves or star anise.

6   Spoon the jam into warm, dry, sterilized jars, then seal and process in a boiling water canner for 10 minutes. Label and date, and refrigerate after opening.

NOTE
❋

This is a thin, softer set jam, but if you would like a firmer set, use gelling sugar (which has pectin added).

QUINCE & STAR ANISE JAM

❧ MAKES 6 JARS (1 CUP/250 ML EACH) • PREPARATION: 30 MINUTES • COOKING: 1½ HOURS ❧

3 pounds (1.5 kg) ripe quinces
4 whole star anise
2 bay leaves

1 tablespoon (15 ml) lemon juice
Grated zest of 1 orange
4½ cups (1.125 L) granulated sugar, warmed

1 2
3 4

1	Peel and core the quinces, then put the peelings and cores into a piece of cheesecloth and tie with string.	2	Finely chop the quinces and put into a pan. Add the star anises, bay leaves, lemon juice, orange zest and 7 cups (1.75 L) of water.	
3	Bring to a boil, then reduce the heat and simmer for 1 hour, until the fruit is soft.	4	Add the sugar and stir over low heat until the sugar has dissolved.	➤

| 5 | Return to a boil and cook, without stirring, for 25 minutes, until the jam reaches setting point. Remove the pan from the heat and remove and discard the star anise, bay leaves and cheese-cloth bag. Stir to remove the scum. | **VARIATION**
❋
You can substitute the star anise with a cinnamon stick or cardamom pods, if you like. |

| 6 | Spoon the jam into warm, dry, sterilized jars, then seal and process in a boiling water canner for 10 minutes. Label and date, and refrigerate after opening. | **TIP**
✼

Quince will discolor quickly when peeled and chopped. To prevent this from happening, rub the peeled quince with a piece of lemon. |

RASPBERRY & LAVENDER JAM

❧ MAKES 7 JARS (1 CUP/250 ML EACH) • PREPARATION: 20 MINUTES • COOKING: 10 MINUTES ❧

3 pounds (1.5 kg) raspberries
4½ cups (1.125 L) granulated sugar,
 warmed
1 lemon, sliced, then put in a piece of
 cheesecloth and tied with string

1 tablespoon (15 ml) lemon juice
1 teaspoon (5 ml) rose water
¼ cup (60 ml) lavender sugar

NOTE:
You can make lavender sugar by putting
2 tablespoons (30 ml) dried lavender
flowers, broken into pieces, into 4 cups (1 L)
of granulated or superfine sugar.

1	Put half the raspberries in a pan and crush. Add remaining raspberries and the white sugar. Stir over low heat until the sugar has dissolved.	2	Add the cheesecloth bag, lemon juice and rose water to the pan. Bring to a boil and cook for 5 minutes for soft jam or 8 minutes for firm jam.
3	Remove from the heat and skim to remove scum. Remove the cheesecloth bag. Leave for 5 minutes. Stir through the lavender sugar until dissolved.	4	Spoon the jam into warm, dry, sterilized jars, then seal and process. Label and date, and refrigerate after opening.

BLUEBERRY JAM

❧ MAKES 5 JARS (1 CUP/250 ML EACH) • PREPARATION: 10 MINUTES • COOKING: 35 MINUTES ❧

2 pounds (1 kg) blueberries
2 tablespoons (30 ml) lemon juice
3¾ cups (925 ml) granulated sugar, warmed

1 2
3 4

1	Rinse the blueberries and allow to dry, then transfer them to a large pan with the lemon juice, sugar and 1 cup (250 ml) of water.	2	Stir over low heat until the sugar dissolves. Boil for 30 minutes, until setting point is reached. Remove from the heat.
3	Put a little jam onto a frozen plate, and if a skin forms when you push your finger through the jam, it is ready. Stir to remove the scum.	4	Spoon the jam into warm, dry, sterilized jars, then seal and process. Label and date, and refrigerate after opening.

GRAPE & GROUND CHERRY JAM

❧ MAKES 4 JARS (1 CUP/250 ML EACH) • PREPARATION: 20 MINUTES • COOKING: 1¼ HOURS ❧

1 pound (500 g) seedless grapes
1 pound (500 g) ground cherries
   (Cape gooseberries)

4½ cups (1.125 L) granulated sugar,
   warmed
2 tablespoons (30 ml) lemon juice

1	Cut the grapes in half. Remove the papery outer layer from the ground cherries and cut them in half as well.	2	Put the grapes, ground cherries and 2 cups (500 ml) of water into a large pan.	
3	Cook for 30 minutes, until the fruit is soft, then mash.	4	Add the sugar and lemon juice and stir over low heat until the sugar has dissolved.	➤

| 5 | Bring to a boil and cook for 30 minutes, until setting point is reached. Remove the pan from the heat. | **VARIATION**
❋
You can substitute the ground cherries with gooseberries when they are in season, if you like. |

| 6 | Spoon the jam into warm, dry, sterilized jars, then seal and process in a boiling water canner for 10 minutes. Label and date, and refrigerate after opening. | **TIP**
If you would like a smooth jam, strain the mixture to remove the seeds before adding the sugar. |

6

MIXED BERRY & VANILLA JAM

MAKES 2½ JARS (1 CUP/250 ML EACH) • PREPARATION: 10 MINUTES • COOKING: 35 MINUTES

2 pounds (1 kg) fresh or frozen mixed berries, such as blueberries, raspberries, blackberries, red currants

4½ cups (1.125 L) granulated sugar, warmed
1 vanilla bean
2 tablespoons (30 ml) lemon juice

1	Put the berries, sugar, vanilla, lemon juice and 1 cup (250 ml) of water into a pan and stir over low heat until the sugar has dissolved.	2	Bring to a boil and cook for 25 minutes, until the jam reaches setting point.
3	Remove from the heat and remove the vanilla bean. Stir to remove the scum.	4	Spoon the jam into warm, dry, sterilized jars, then seal and process. Label and date, and refrigerate after opening.

STRAWBERRY JAM

❋ MAKES 5 JARS (1 CUP/250 ML EACH) • PREPARATION: 20 MINUTES + MACERATING OVERNIGHT • COOKING: 30 MINUTES ❋

2 pounds (1 kg) strawberries, rinsed, dried and hulled

4 cups (1 L) granulated sugar, warmed

Juice of 1 small lemon (about 2 tablespoons/ 30 ml lemon juice)

1 2
3 4

1	Cut half the strawberries in half, leaving the remaining strawberries whole.	2	Put the strawberries, sugar and lemon juice into a bowl, cover with parchment paper and set aside overnight.	
3	The next day, put the strawberries and liquid into a large pan and stir over low heat until the sugar has dissolved.	4	Bring to a boil and cook for about 25 minutes, until the jam has reached setting point.	➤

5	Remove the pan from the heat. Put a little jam onto a frozen plate, and if a skin forms when you push your finger through the jam, it is ready. Stir to remove the scum, then leave for 10 minutes for the fruit to settle (this will stop the strawberries from all rising to the top of the jar).	**VARIATION** ❋ Frozen strawberries can be used to make this recipe — just cook them from frozen.

| 6 | Spoon the jam into warm, dry, sterilized jars, then seal and process in a boiling water canner for 10 minutes. Label and date, and refrigerate the jam after opening. This jam is delicious served with biscuits (see recipe 26). | **TIP** ✻
Chop the strawberries into small pieces if you prefer a smoother jam. |

BLACK GRAPE & MERLOT JAM

❧ MAKES 5 JARS (1 CUP/250 ML EACH) • PREPARATION: 20 MINUTES + MACERATING OVERNIGHT • COOKING: 1 HOUR ❧

3 pounds (1.5 kg) seedless black grapes,
    washed and dried
2 tablespoons (30 ml) lemon juice

1 cup (250 ml) Merlot wine
3¾ cups (925 ml) granulated sugar, warmed

1 2
3 4

1	Put the grapes, lemon juice, Merlot and sugar into a non-metallic bowl, cover with parchment paper and leave for several hours or overnight.	2	Transfer the mix to a pan and stir over low heat until the sugar dissolves. Boil until thick. Skim to remove scum. Boil until setting point.
3	Remove from the heat. Put a little jam onto a frozen plate, and if a skin forms when you push your finger through the jam, it is ready.	4	Spoon the jam into warm, dry, sterilized jars, then seal and process. Label and date, and refrigerate after opening.

RHUBARB & GINGER JAM

➤ MAKES 10 JARS (1 CUP/250 ML EACH) • PREPARATION: 15 MINUTES + CHILLING OVERNIGHT • COOKING: 20 MINUTES ➤

1¾ ounces (50 g) fresh ginger
1 lemon
3 pounds (1.5 kg) rhubarb, trimmed and
   chopped

2 tablespoons (30 ml) lemon juice
6¾ cups (1.675 L) granulated sugar, warmed
5 ounces (150 g) crystallized ginger, chopped

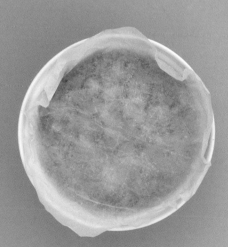

1	Slice the ginger. Remove the skin and pith from the lemon and remove the seeds.	2	Put the ginger slices and lemon skin and seeds into a piece of cheesecloth and tie with string.	
3	Put the rhubarb, lemon juice and sugar into a non-metallic bowl and mix to combine.	4	Cover with parchment paper and chill overnight in the refrigerator.	➤

5 6
7 8

5	The next day, uncover and transfer the mixture to a large pan.	6	Add the cheesecloth bag and stir over low heat until the sugar has dissolved. Boil until thick and glossy. Skim the surface to remove any scum.
7	Remove the cheesecloth bag and stir in the chopped crystallized ginger. Return to a boil and cook until the jam reaches setting point.	8	Remove from the heat. Put a little jam onto a frozen plate, and if a skin forms when you push your finger through the jam, it is ready.

Spoon the jam into warm, dry, sterilized jars, then seal and process in a boiling water canner for 10 minutes. Label and date, and refrigerate after opening.

VARIATION
*

For a deeper red color, add some strawberries to the jam.

SPICED PLUM JAM

❧ MAKES 6 JARS (1 CUP/250 ML EACH) • PREPARATION: 20 MINUTES • COOKING: 50 MINUTES ❦

2 cinnamon sticks
4 cloves
1 vanilla bean
Zest and juice of 1 orange

2 pounds (1 kg) plums
4½ cups (1.125 L) granulated sugar, warmed
2 tablespoons (30 ml) lemon juice

1 2
3 4

1	Put all the spices and orange zest into a spice basket or tea ball.	2	Chop the plums, then put them into a pan with 2 cups (500 ml) of water and the spice basket.	
3	Cook for 25 minutes, until the plums are soft and pulpy.	4	Add the sugar and lemon juice and stir over low heat until the sugar has dissolved.	➤

5	Bring to a boil and cook for 20 minutes, until thick and the jam reaches setting point. Remove the spice basket.	**VARIATION** ❊ You can use damson plums to make this recipe when they are in season.

6 Spoon the jam into warm, dry, sterilized jars, then seal and process in a boiling water canner for 10 minutes. Label and date, and refrigerate after opening.

NOTE
❋
Any plums may be used to make this recipe — yellow-flesh plums will still give you a vibrant red tone.

PINEAPPLE & PEPPERCORN JAM

✦ MAKES 6 JARS (1 CUP/250 ML EACH) • PREPARATION: 20 MINUTES • COOKING: 50 MINUTES ✦

2 lemons
1 medium ripe pineapple, cored and
    chopped

1 tablespoon (15 ml) pink peppercorns,
    lightly crushed
4½ cups (1.125 L) granulated sugar, warmed

NOTE:
The pineapple should be ripe but not
overripe or it will affect the setting of
the jam.

1 2
3 4

1	Remove the peel and pith from the lemons and put into a piece of cheesecloth along with the seeds, then tie with string. Squeeze the lemons and reserve the juice.	2	Put the pineapple, peppercorns, cheesecloth bag and 4 cups (1 L) of water into a large pan and cook for 30 minutes, until soft. Mash.
3	Add the sugar and lemon juice and stir over low heat until the sugar has dissolved. Boil until the jam reaches setting point.	4	Remove the cheesecloth bag. Spoon the jam into warm, dry, sterilized jars, then seal and process. Label and date, and refrigerate after opening.

SPICED FIG & WALNUT JAM

→ MAKES 6 JARS (1 CUP/250 ML EACH) • PREPARATION: 20 MINUTES + MACERATING OVERNIGHT • COOKING: 15 MINUTES ←

2 pounds (1 kg) fresh figs
3¾ cups (925 ml) granulated sugar, warmed
1 tablespoon (15 ml) grated orange zest

2 tablespoons (30 ml) lemon juice
2 cinnamon sticks
4 cardamom pods, lightly crushed

3 whole cloves
3½ ounces (100 g) walnuts, about 1 cup
    (250 ml), roughly chopped

1	Chop the figs and put into a non-metallic bowl with the sugar, orange zest and lemon juice.	2	Put the spices into a piece of cheesecloth, tie with string and add to the fig mixture. Mix, cover and leave for several hours or overnight.	
3	Uncover and transfer the mixture to a large pan.	4	Stir the mixture over low heat until the sugar has dissolved. Boil until the jam reaches setting point.	➤

5	Remove the cheesecloth bag and stir in the walnuts.	**VARIATION** ❋ Try substituting the walnuts with the same amount of pistachio nuts or hazelnuts, if you like.

6	Spoon the jam into warm, dry, sterilized jars, then seal and process in a boiling water canner for 10 minutes. Label and date, and refrigerate after opening.	**NOTE** ❋ This is quite a thick jam, so make sure the figs are chopped into quite small pieces and the walnuts are finely chopped.

SQUASH & CINNAMON JAM

❧ MAKES ABOUT 7 JARS (1 CUP/250 ML EACH) • PREPARATION: 30 MINUTES • COOKING: 40 MINUTES ❧

3 pounds (1.5 k) winter squash
1 cup (250 ml) orange juice
2 vanilla beans, cut in half lengthwise
2 tablespoons (30 ml) lemon juice

2 cinnamon sticks
1 teaspoon (5 ml) ground cinnamon
4½ cups (1.125 L) granulated sugar, warmed

1	Peel and grate the squash into a large, non-metallic bowl.	2	Add the orange juice, vanilla halves, lemon juice, cinnamon and mix well.	3	Transfer to a pan and add 2 cups (500 ml) of water. Cook until soft.
4	Add the sugar and stir over low heat until the sugar has dissolved. Boil, stirring frequently, for 15 minutes.	5	Remove the vanilla beans, then boil until the jam reaches setting point. Remove from the heat.	6	Spoon the jam into warm, dry, sterilized jars; seal and process. Label and date, and refrigerate after opening.

CHOCOLATE & FRUIT JAM

❧ MAKES 8 JARS (1 CUP/250 ML EACH) • PREPARATION: 30 MINUTES • COOKING: 1¼ HOURS ❧

2 pounds (1 kg) black plums
1 pound (500 g) blueberries
1 pound (500 g) raspberries
2 tablespoons (30 ml) lemon juice

8 ounces (250 g) dark bittersweet chocolate,
  about 70% cocoa solids
6¾ cups (1.675 L) granulated sugar, warmed

1 2
3 4

1	Cut the plums in half, remove the pits and cut the plums into wedges. Put the fruit into a pan with 4 cups (1 L) of water.	2	Bring to a boil, reduce the heat and simmer until soft. Add the remaining ingredients and stir over low heat to dissolve the sugar.
3	Bring to a boil and cook for 20 minutes, stirring regularly, until the jam reaches setting point. Remove the pan from the heat.	4	Spoon the jam into warm, dry, sterilized jars, then seal and process. Label and date, and refrigerate after opening.

PEACH & PASSION FRUIT JAM

❧ MAKES 6 JARS (1 CUP/250 ML EACH) • PREPARATION: 20 MINUTES • COOKING: 30 MINUTES ❦

2½ pounds (1.2 kg) peaches
8 passion fruits

3¾ cups (925 ml) granulated sugar, warmed
2 tablespoons (30 ml) lemon juice

1 2
3 4

1	Peel the peaches (see notes), if you like, remove pits and cut peaches into wedges. Squeeze passion fruits to give 1 cup (250 ml) of juice.	2	Put the peaches, passion fruit juice and 1 cup (250 ml) of water into a large pan and cook for 10 minutes, until peaches are soft.	
3	Add the sugar and lemon juice and stir over low heat until the sugar has dissolved.	4	Bring to a boil and cook for about 10 minutes, stirring a couple of times, until the jam reaches setting point.	➤

| 5 | Remove the pan from the heat. Put a little jam onto a frozen plate, and if a skin forms when you push your finger through the jam, it is ready. | **VARIATION**
❋
Use nectarines or apricots instead of the peaches, if you prefer. |

| 6 | Spoon the jam into warm, dry, sterilized jars, then seal and process in a boiling water canner for 10 minutes. Label and date, and refrigerate after opening. | **NOTES**
❋
To peel peaches, cut a small x in the top of each one, then put them in a bowl of hot water and leave until the skins start to come away. Transfer to a bowl of iced water and, when cool, peel off the skins.

This jam is a soft set and makes a delicious sauce — use gelling sugar if you prefer a thicker jam. |

WATERMELON & GERANIUM JAM

➤ MAKES 4 JARS (1 CUP/250 ML EACH) • PREPARATION: 20 MINUTES • COOKING: 30 MINUTES ➤

1 pound (500 g) red apples, peeled, cored
   and chopped
4 to 6 sweet-smelling rose geranium leaves

2 pounds (1 kg) seedless watermelon,
   chopped
3¾ cups (925 ml) granulated sugar, warmed
2 tablespoons (30 ml) lemon juice

1 2
3 4

1	Put apple cores, seeds and geranium leaves into a piece of cheesecloth and tie with string. Put apples and melon into a large pan and cook until soft.	2	Add the sugar and lemon juice and stir over low heat until the sugar has dissolved.	
3	Remove the pan from the heat and, using a handheld blender, blitz until smooth.	4	Return the pan to the heat and add the cheesecloth bag.	➤

| 5 | Bring to a boil, stirring regularly, for 15 minutes, until the jam reaches setting point. Remove the cheesecloth bag, then remove the pan from the heat. | **VARIATION**
❋

Substitute the geranium leaves with some fresh rose petals, if you like. Make sure neither has been sprayed with pesticides, or wash thoroughly. |

| 6 | Spoon the jam into warm, dry, sterilized jars, then seal and process in a boiling water canner for 10 minutes. Label and date, and refrigerate after opening. | **TIP** ❋
Try to find seedless, brightly colored, fragrant watermelon, as it will have a big impact on the final color of this jam. |

APRICOT, NUT & SAFFRON JAM

❖ MAKES ABOUT 10 JARS (1 CUP/250 ML EACH) • PREPARATION: 15 MINUTES + SOAKING OVERNIGHT • COOKING: 50 MINUTES ❖

1½ pounds (750 g) dried apricots
Generous pinch of saffron threads
2 bay leaves
Zest of 1 orange

5⅔ cups (1.4 L) granulated sugar
2 tablespoons (30 ml) lemon juice
½ cup (125 ml) flaked almonds

1 2
3 4

1	Put the apricots in a non-metallic bowl, add the saffron, bay leaves, orange zest and 8 cups (2 L) of hot water, cover and leave overnight.	2	Remove the bay leaves and, using a handheld blender, blitz until smooth. Transfer the apricot mixture to a pan.
3	Add the sugar and lemon juice and stir until the sugar dissolves, then bring to a boil and cook for 25 minutes.	4	Stir in the almonds. Boil until the jam reaches setting point, then spoon into jars, seal and process. Label and date, then chill after opening.

MANGO & LEMONGRASS JAM

❧ MAKES 6 JARS (1 CUP/250 ML EACH) • PREPARATION: 20 MINUTES • COOKING: 40 MINUTES ❧

3 pounds (1.5 kg) mangoes (not too ripe),
 chopped
Grated zest of 3 limes
3 tablespoons (45 ml) chopped lemongrass

2 tablespoons (30 ml) lemon juice
6¾ cups pounds (1.675 L) granulated sugar,
 warmed

1 2
3 4

1	Put the mangoes, lime zest, lemongrass, lemon juice and ½ cup (125 ml) of water into a pan. Boil for 20 minutes, until the mangoes are soft.	2	Remove the pan from the heat and mash until smooth.
3	Add the sugar and stir over low heat until the sugar has dissolved. Boil for 15 minutes, until the jam reaches setting point.	4	Remove the pan from the heat and spoon the jam into warm, dry, sterilized jars; seal and process. Label and date, then refrigerate after opening.

RHUBARB & STRAWBERRY JAM

❧ MAKES 6 JARS (1 CUP/250 ML EACH) • PREPARATION: 20 MINUTES • COOKING: 50 MINUTES ❧

2 pounds (1 kg) rhubarb, trimmed and
   chopped
1 pound (500 g) strawberries, hulled
12 sprigs mint, tied with string and
   lightly crushed

2 tablespoons (30 ml) lemon juice
5⅔ cups (1.4 L) granulated sugar, warmed
1 cup (250 ml) pure maple syrup
1½ teaspoons (7 ml) cracked black pepper

1 2
3 4

1	Put the rhubarb and 1 cup (250 ml) of water into a large pan and cook until soft.	2	Add the strawberries, mint, lemon juice and sugar and stir over low heat until the sugar has dissolved.
3	Bring to a boil and cook for 30 minutes, until the jam reaches setting point. Remove the mint and add the maple syrup and black pepper.	4	Remove the pan from the heat and spoon the jam into warm, dry, sterilized jars; seal and process. Label and date, then refrigerate after opening.

SEEDLESS RASPBERRY JAM

❧ MAKES 4 JARS (1 CUP/250 ML EACH) • PREPARATION: 20 MINUTES • COOKING: 20 MINUTES ❧

2 pounds (1 kg) raspberries
Juice of 2 small lemons
3¾ cups (925 ml) granulated sugar, warmed

1 2
3 4

1	Crush the raspberries in a blender and then press through a sieve to remove the seeds.	2	Put the pulp into a large pan with the remaining ingredients and stir over low heat until the sugar has dissolved.	
3	Bring to a boil and cook until the jam is thick and glossy. Skim to remove any scum, then boil again until the jam reaches setting point.	4	Put a little jam onto a frozen plate, and if a skin forms when you push your finger through the jam, it is ready.	➤

| 5 | Spoon the jam into warm, dry, sterilized jars, then seal and process in a boiling water canner for 10 minutes. Label and date, and refrigerate after opening. | **VARIATIONS**
※
Try making this jam with vanilla sugar for a more aromatic jam. You could also add the zest of 1 orange to the jam, if you like. |

| 6 | This jam is particularly delicious as a filling for butterfly cakes. | **NOTE**
❋
If you are very short of time, omit straining the raspberries. |

QUINCE & ELDERFLOWER JAM

➤ MAKES 4 JARS (1 CUP/250 ML EACH) • PREPARATION: 20 MINUTES • COOKING: 1¼ HOURS ➤

2 pounds (1 kg) quinces
1 pound (500 g) green apples
4½ cups (1.125 L) granulated sugar, warmed

2 tablespoons (30 ml) lemon juice
½ cup (125 ml) elderflower cordial

1 2
3 4

1	Peel, core and cut the quinces into pieces. Peel and core the apples and cut into pieces.	2	Put the quinces, apples and 4 cups (1 L) of water into a large pan.	
3	Bring to a boil and cook for 50 minutes, until the quinces are soft.	4	Add the sugar, lemon juice and elderflower cordial and stir over low heat until the sugar has dissolved.	➤

5	Bring to a boil and cook for 20 minutes, until thick and the jam reaches setting point. Remove the pan from the heat.	**VARIATION** ❈ If fresh elderflowers are available, wrap them in a piece of cheesecloth, tie with string and add them with the quinces.

| 6 | Spoon the jam into warm, dry, sterilized jars, then seal and process in a boiling water canner for 10 minutes. Label and date, and refrigerate after opening. | **TIP**
❈
Before peeling the quinces, remove the fuzz from the skin with wet paper towels. |

BANANA & PISTACHIO JAM

➤ MAKES 6 JARS (1 CUP/250 ML EACH) • PREPARATION: 15 MINUTES • COOKING: 40 MINUTES ➤

2 pounds (1 kg) bananas, sliced
½ cup (125 ml) lemon juice

4½ cups (1.125 L) granulated sugar, warmed
½ cup (125 ml) pistachio nuts, roughly
    chopped

1 2
3 4

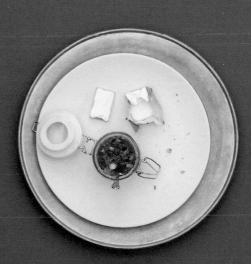

1	Put the bananas, lemon juice, sugar and 1 cup (250 ml) of water into a large pan and stir over low heat until the sugar has dissolved.	2	Bring to a boil and cook, stirring regularly, for 30 minutes, until the jam is pulpy and reaches setting point.
3	Stir in the pistachios, then remove the pan from the heat.	4	Spoon the jam into warm, dry, sterilized jars, then seal and process. Label and date, and refrigerate after opening.

BLACKBERRY JAM

➤ MAKES 4 JARS (1 CUP/250 ML EACH) • PREPARATION: 10 MINUTES • COOKING: 50 MINUTES ➤

2 pounds (1 kg) blackberries
2 tablespoons (30 ml) lemon juice
4½ cups (1.125 L) granulated sugar, warmed

1 2
3 4

1	Put the blackberries, lemon juice, sugar and ½ cup (125 ml) of water into a large pan and stir over low heat until the sugar has dissolved.	2	Bring to a boil and cook for 40 minutes, until the jam reaches setting point.
3	Remove from the heat. Put a little jam onto a frozen plate, and if a skin forms when you push your finger through the jam, it is ready.	4	Spoon the jam into warm, dry, sterilized jars, then seal and process. Label and date, and refrigerate after opening.

TOMATO & PASSION FRUIT JAM

❧ MAKES 9 JARS (1 CUP/250 ML EACH) • PREPARATION: 30 MINUTES • COOKING: 50 MINUTES ❧

1 pound (500 g) ripe tomatoes, chopped
2 pounds (1 kg) nectarines, chopped
6¾ cups (1.675 L) granulated sugar, warmed

Juice of 1 lemon
6 passion fruits

1 2
3 4

1	Put the tomatoes, nectarines and 4 cups (1 L) of water into a large pan and boil gently until the fruit is soft.	2	Remove from the heat and, using a handheld blender, blitz to a puree.
3	Add the sugar and lemon juice and stir over low heat to dissolve sugar. Boil for 15 minutes. Add passion fruits and cook until setting point.	4	Spoon the jam into warm, dry, sterilized jars, then seal and process. Label and date, and refrigerate after opening.

FIG, MUSCAT & ROSEMARY JAM

➤ MAKES 9 JARS (1 CUP/250 ML EACH) • PREPARATION: 20 MINUTES • COOKING: 40 MINUTES ◆

2 pounds (1 kg) dried figs, chopped into
    small pieces
1½ cups (375 ml) Muscat wine
6 sprigs rosemary

1 teaspoon (5 ml) ground cinnamon
4½ cups (1.125 L) granulated sugar, warmed
3 tablespoons (45 ml) lemon juice

1 2
3 4

1	Put the figs, Muscat, rosemary, cinnamon and ½ cup (125 ml) of water into a large pan and bring to a boil.	2	Reduce the heat and simmer until soft. Add the sugar and lemon juice and stir over low heat until the sugar has dissolved.
3	Bring to a boil and cook until the jam reaches setting point. Remove the rosemary, then remove the pan from the heat.	4	Spoon the jam into warm, dry, sterilized jars, then seal and process. Label and date, and refrigerate after opening.

BISCUITS

❧ MAKES 20 • PREPARATION: 20 MINUTES • COOKING: 15 MINUTES ❧

4 cups (1 L) self-rising flour, sifted
½ teaspoon (2 ml) salt

1 cup (250 ml) milk
1½ cups (375 ml) table cream (18%)

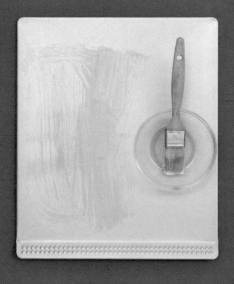

1 2
3 4

1	Preheat the oven to 500°F (250°C). Oil a non-stick baking sheet.	2	Sift the flour into a large bowl, then stir in the salt and make a well in the center.	
3	Using a flat-bladed knife, gradually stir in the milk and cream until the mixture comes together.	4	Turn out onto a lightly floured surface and knead gently until the mixture forms a soft dough.	➤

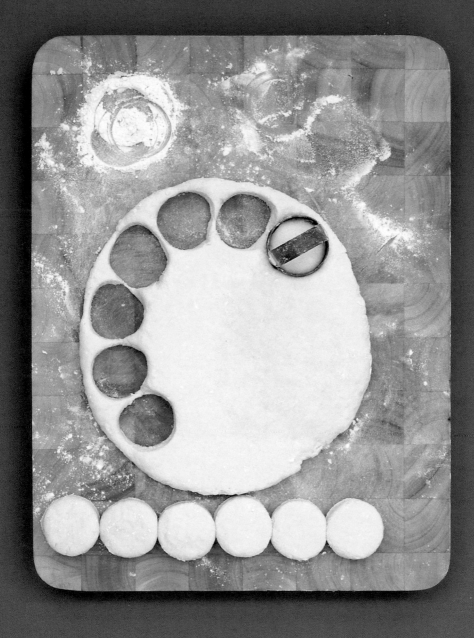

5	Roll out the dough to ¾ inch (2 cm) thick, then, using a 2-inch (5 cm) round cookie cutter, cut out rounds from the dough. Press the scraps back together to get as many circles from the dough as you can.	**VARIATION** ❋ Try adding some chopped pitted dates or raisins to the dry ingredients.

| 6 | Place the circles onto the prepared baking sheet and bake for 12 to 15 minutes, until golden and risen. | **TIP** ❋

Wrap the warm biscuits in a clean tea towel to help keep them warm and moist. |

WHITE BREAD

❧ MAKES 1 LOAF • PREPARATION: 1 HOUR + RISING TIME • COOKING: 40 MINUTES ❧

1 7-g (¼ ounce) package instant yeast
1 teaspoon (5 ml) superfine sugar
4 cups (1 L) white bread flour

1 tablespoon (15 ml) granulated sugar
1 teaspoon (5 ml) salt
¼ cup (60 ml) olive oil

PRELIMINARY:
Preheat the oven to 415°F (210°C).

1   2   3
4   5   6

1	Combine the yeast, superfine sugar and ½ cup (125 ml) of warm water; stir. Leave in a warm place until foamy.	2	Sift the flour into a large bowl and stir in the granulated sugar and salt. Make a well in the center.	3	Add the yeast, then gradually add the oil and 1 cup (250 ml) of warm water; mix until a dough comes together.
4	Turn the dough out onto a lightly floured surface and knead for 10 minutes, until smooth.	5	Put the dough into an oiled bowl, cover with a damp tea towel and let stand in a warm place until doubled in size.	6	Punch the dough down and knead for a further 1 minute.

| 7 | Shape the dough into a loaf and put into a lightly oiled loaf tin. Cover with a damp tea towel and stand in a warm, draft-free place for about 45 minutes, until doubled in size. | **VARIATION**
❄
If you would like to make fresh bread rolls, divide the dough into 16 even-sized pieces and roll into balls. Allow to rise then bake for 20 minutes. |

8	Bake the loaf for 10 minutes, then reduce the temperature to 350°F (180°C) and bake for a further 30 minutes. The base of the bread should sound hollow when tapped after it has been removed from the pan.

NOTES
❈

If the yeast mixture does not become foamy after 10 minutes, throw it out and start again.

Do not rush step 4, as this is where you get the rise in the bread.

KIWIFRUIT & JASMINE JAM

❧ MAKES 6 JARS (1 CUP/250 ML EACH) • PREPARATION: 30 MINUTES • COOKING: 1 HOUR ❧

2 pounds (1 kg) kiwifruit, peeled and
  chopped
1 pound (500 g) apples, peeled, cored and
  chopped

Rind, pith and seeds of 1 lemon
2 jasmine tea bags
4½ cups (1.125 L) granulated sugar, warmed

1 2
3 4

1	Peel the fruit and chop into pieces. Wrap the cores, lemon rind, pith, seeds and tea bags in a piece of cheesecloth and tie with string.	2	Put the apples, kiwifruit, the cheesecloth bag and 4 cups (1 L) of water into a large pan and boil until soft.
3	Add the sugar and stir over low heat until the sugar dissolves. Boil for 30 minutes, until setting point. Skim to remove any scum.	4	Remove from the heat and spoon the jam into warm, dry, sterilized jars, then seal and process. Label and date, and refrigerate after opening.

CURDS, BUTTERS, FRUIT CHEESES & CHOCOLATE SPREADS

2

LEMON CURD

❧ MAKES 2½ CUPS (625 ML)• PREPARATION: 20 MINUTES • COOKING: 30 MINUTES ❧

2 tablespoons (30 ml) finely grated
   lemon zest
¾ cup (175 ml) lemon juice
¾ cup (175 ml) unsalted butter, softened

1⅓ cups (325 ml) superfine sugar
12 egg yolks

NOTE:
Do not allow the water in the pan to boil
in step 3.

1 2
3 4

1	Put the lemon zest, lemon juice, butter and sugar in a non-metallic heatproof bowl.	2	Place the bowl over a pan of simmering water, making sure the base of the bowl does not touch the water. Stir until the sugar dissolves.
3	Add the egg yolks and stir constantly for about 15 to 20 minutes, until the curd coats the back of a spoon.	4	Strain the mixture and reheat gently. Pour into clean, dry, sterilized jars to the top. Seal while hot, label and date, then chill for up to 2 months.

PASSION FRUIT CURD

MAKES ABOUT 2¾ CUPS (675 ML) • PREPARATION: 15 MINUTES • COOKING: 30 MINUTES

4 eggs
2 egg yolks
1⅓ cups (325 ml) superfine sugar
1 teaspoon (5 ml) grated orange zest
2 teaspoons (10 ml) grated lemon zest
2 tablespoons (30 ml) lemon juice
1 cup (250 ml) passion fruit pulp
⅞ cup (200 ml) butter, chopped into pieces

NOTES:
Make sure the base of the bowl is not touching the water in step 3. Do not allow the water to boil in step 4.

1	Whisk the eggs and egg yolks, then strain into a non-metallic heatproof bowl.	2	Add the sugar, orange and lemon zest, lemon juice, passion fruit pulp and butter.	
3	Place the bowl over a pan of simmering water and stir until the sugar dissolves and the butter melts.	4	Stir constantly for 15 to 20 minutes, until the curd coats the back of a spoon.	➤

| 5 | Pour the curd into clean, dry, sterilized jars to the top and seal while hot. | **TIP**
❋
If you prefer a smoother curd, strain the passion fruit pulp to remove the seeds. |

| 6 | Label and date the jars, and refrigerate for up to 2 months. | **NOTE**
❋
This curd will soften on returning to room temperature, so if you want it to hold its shape, take it out of the refrigerator just before serving. |

ORANGE, LIME & COCONUT CURD

❖ MAKES ABOUT 2½ CUPS (625 ML) • PREPARATION: 20 MINUTES • COOKING: 45 MINUTES ❖

1½ tablespoons (22 ml) finely grated
    orange zest
1 tablespoon (15 ml) grated lime zest
1 cup (250 ml) fresh orange juice
½ cup (125 ml) coconut cream

⅞ cup (200 ml) unsalted butter, chopped
    into pieces
1⅓ cups (325 ml) superfine sugar
12 egg yolks

NOTE:
Do not allow the water in the pan to boil
in step 3.

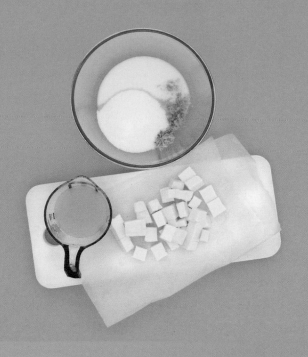

1	Put the orange and lime zest, orange juice, coconut cream, butter and sugar in a non-metallic heatproof bowl.	2	Place the bowl over a pan of simmering water, making sure the base of the bowl does not touch the water. Stir until the sugar dissolves.
3	Add the egg yolks and stir constantly for about 30 to 40 minutes, until the curd coats the back of a spoon.	4	Strain the mixture and reheat gently. Pour into clean, dry, sterilized jars. Seal while hot, label and date, then refrigerate for up to 2 months.

MANGO & LIME CURD

❧ MAKES 2½ CUPS (625 ML) • PREPARATION: 20 MINUTES • COOKING: 30 MINUTES ❧

1 cup (250 ml) fresh mango puree
2 tablespoons (30 ml) finely grated lime zest
⅓ cup (75 ml) lime juice
¾ cup (175 ml) unsalted butter, softened

1⅓ cups (325 ml) superfine sugar
12 egg yolks

NOTE:
Do not allow the water in the pan to boil
in step 3.

1 2
3 4

1	Put the mango puree, lime zest, lime juice, butter and sugar in a non-metallic heatproof bowl.	2	Place the bowl over a pan of simmering water, making sure the base of the bowl does not touch the water. Stir until the sugar dissolves.
3	Add the egg yolks and stir constantly for about 15 to 20 minutes, until the curd coats the back of a spoon.	4	Strain the mixture and reheat gently. Pour into clean, dry, sterilized jars and seal while hot. Label and date, then refrigerate for up to 2 months.

RASPBERRY CURD

➤ MAKES 2¾ CUPS (675 ML) • PREPARATION: 15 MINUTES • COOKING: 30 MINUTES ➤

6 ounces (170 g) raspberries
4 eggs
2 egg yolks
1⅓ cups (325 ml) superfine sugar
1 teaspoon (5 ml) grated orange zest

2 teaspoons (10 ml) grated lemon zest
2 tablespoons (30 ml) lemon juice
⅞ cup (200 ml) unsalted butter, chopped
  into pieces

NOTES:
Make sure the base of the bowl is not
touching the water in step 3. Do not allow
the water in the pan to boil in step 4.

1 2
3 4

1	Process the raspberries in a blender or food processor to form a smooth puree.	2	Whisk the eggs and egg yolks, then strain into a heatproof bowl. Add the sugar, citrus zest, lemon juice and butter.
3	Place the bowl over a pan of simmering water and stir until the sugar dissolves and the butter melts.	4	Continue to stir constantly for about 15 to 20 minutes, until the curd coats the back of a spoon. ➤

5	Strain the raspberry curd through a sieve.	**TIP** Try adding lightly crushed raspberry puree to the curd after it has been cooked.

| 6 | Pour the curd into clean, dry, sterilized jars to the top and seal while hot, then label and date. Keep in the refrigerator for up to 2 months. Raspberry curd is delicious folded through crushed meringues and whipped cream. | **VARIATIONS**
❋
You can make this recipe using either strawberries or blackberries instead of the raspberries, if you prefer. |

BUTTERNUT SQUASH BUTTER

❧ MAKES ABOUT 2½ CUPS (625 ML) • PREPARATION: 30 MINUTES • COOKING: 50 MINUTES ❧

2 pounds (1 kg) butternut squash, peeled
    and cut into cubes
Generous pinch of saffron threads

About 2¼ cups (550 ml) granulated sugar,
    warmed
1 teaspoon (5 ml) ground cinnamon

1 2
3 4

1	Put the butternut squash into a pan and boil until the squash is soft.	2	Meanwhile, put the saffron into a small heatproof bowl, cover with 1 tablespoon (15 ml) hot water and leave for 10 minutes.	
3	Strain the squash through a sieve into a bowl. Measure to calculate how much sugar you will need — 2 cups (500 ml) of puree will need 2 cups (500 ml) of sugar.	4	Put the puree, sugar and saffron, with its liquid, and cinnamon into a pan and stir over low heat to dissolve the sugar.	➤

| 5 | Bring to a boil and cook, stirring, for 30 minutes, until the mixture is thick and holds its shape when spooned onto a cold plate. | **TIP**
✳
The squash butter can be put into an ice cube tray and chilled until firm, then served with cheese and crackers. |

| 6 | Spoon the butter into clean, dry, sterilized jars and seal while hot. Label and date the jars. | **NOTE** ❋
Allow the butter to stand in a cool, dark place for 2 days before eating, then use within 3 months. |

RHUBARB & APPLE BUTTER

❧ MAKES 2½ CUPS (625 ML) • PREPARATION: 30 MINUTES • COOKING: 50 MINUTES ❧

1½ pounds (750 g) rhubarb, chopped
8 ounces (250 g) green apples, peeled,
   cored and chopped
2 teaspoons (10 ml) rose water

About 2¼ cups (550 ml) granulated sugar,
   warmed
3 tablespoons (45 ml) lemon juice

1 2
3 4

1	Put the rhubarb, apples, 1 teaspoon (5 ml) of rosewater and ¾ cup (175 ml) of water in a pan. Boil for 20 minutes, until the fruit is very soft.	2	Transfer the fruit to a bowl and mash until smooth.	
3	Strain through a sieve into a bowl. Measure the puree and add along with an equal amount of sugar to a clean pan.	4	Add the lemon juice and the remaining rose water. Stir over low heat to dissolve the sugar.	➤

| 5 | Bring to a boil and cook, stirring, for 10 to 15 minutes, until the mixture is thick and holds its shape when spooned onto a cold plate. | **TIP**
❋
The butter can be spread into a pan, left to set and then cut out with shaped cutters and rolled in sugar. |

6	Spoon the butter into clean, dry, sterilized jars and seal while hot. Label and date.	**NOTE** ❋ Allow to stand in a cool, dark place for 2 days before eating, then use within 3 months.

MANGO, CHILI & LIME BUTTER

❧ MAKES 2½ CUPS (625 ML) • PREPARATION: 30 MINUTES • COOKING: 50 MINUTES + COOLING TIME ❧

3 pounds (1.5 kg) mangoes, pitted and
   roughly chopped (2 pounds/1 kg pieces)
2¼–3⅓ cups (550–825 ml) granulated
   sugar, warmed

1–2 large red chili peppers, seeded and
   thinly sliced
1 tablespoon (15 ml) finely grated lime zest

1 2
3 4

1	Put the mango into a pan, add enough water to just cover and bring to a boil. Reduce the heat and simmer until soft and pulpy. Cool.	2	Transfer the mango to a blender and blitz until smooth.	
3	Measure the puree and add along with an equal amount of sugar to a clean pan. Add the chilies and lime zest.	4	Cook, stirring occasionally, until the mixture is thick and glossy (see tip on the next page).	➤

5
Pour the mixture into clean, dry, sterilized jars to the top and seal while hot, then label and date. Keep in the refrigerator for up to 2 months.

TIP
❋

The butter is ready when you can drag a wooden spoon along the bottom of the pan and it holds for several seconds before forming together again.

6

For the best flavor, allow the butter to stand for 4 to 6 weeks before eating, then consume within a year.

NOTE
❋

You can pour the mixture into molds lined with waxed or parchment paper and cover with melted food-grade paraffin wax.

BLACKBERRY & WINE CHEESE

➤ MAKES 30 SQUARES • PREPARATION: 30 MINUTES • COOKING: 50 MINUTES + COOLING & CHILLING TIME ➤

2 pounds (1 kg) blackberries
2 apples, peeled and chopped
2 tablespoons (30 ml) lemon juice

½ cup (125 ml) red wine
Gelling sugar (see step 3), warmed

1	Cook the fruit, lemon juice, wine and ¼ cup (60 ml) of water until fruit is soft. Cool.	2	Push the fruit through a sieve, then measure the puree.	3	Add an equal amount of sugar to a clean pan with the puree. Cook until thick.
4	Spoon the cheese into a pan lined with parchment or waxed paper. Cover with paper and chill until firm.	5	Remove the cheese from the pan and cut into shapes.	6	Roll the shapes in sugar. For the best flavor, allow 4 to 6 weeks to dry out slightly before eating.

QUINCE CHEESE

❧ MAKES 1 (7 X 10½ INCHES / 17 X 27CM) PAN • PREPARATION: 15 MINUTES • COOKING: 2–3 HOURS + COOLING TIME ❧

2 pounds (1 kg) quinces, unpeeled and
    roughly chopped
About 2¼–3⅓ cups (550–825 ml)
    granulated sugar

1 2
3 4

1	Put the quince into a pan, add enough water to just cover and bring to a boil. Reduce the heat and simmer for 1 hour, until soft. Cool.	2	Push the quince through a sieve or food mill.	
3	Measure the puree and add an equal amount of sugar to a clean pan with the quince puree.	4	Cook, stirring occasionally, until the mixture is thick and glossy.	➤

			TIP ❋
5	Pour the mixture into a pan lined with parchment or waxed paper.		The cheese is ready when you can drag a wooden spoon along the bottom of the pan and it holds for several seconds before coming together again.

6	Cover with waxed or parchment paper and store in the refrigerator until firm. For the best flavor, allow 4 to 6 weeks of time to pass before eating, then consume within a year.	**NOTE** ❋ You can pour the cheese into molds, greased or lined with waxed or parchment paper, and cover with melted food-grade paraffin wax.

CHOCOLATE-HAZELNUT SPREAD

❧ MAKES 1¼ CUPS (300 ML) • PREPARATION: 10 MINUTES + 15 MINUTES INFUSING • COOKING: 15 MINUTES ❧

1¼ cups (300 ml) heavy cream (36%)
5 ounces (150 g), about 1 cup (250 ml), toasted hazelnuts, chopped

10 ounces (300 g) dark or milk chocolate, chopped
2 teaspoons (10 ml) sunflower oil

NOTE:
If you want a crunchy spread, add half the strained hazelnuts back into the spread.

1	Put the cream and chopped hazelnuts into a pan, bring to a simmer and cook for 10 minutes. Remove and allow to infuse for 15 minutes.	2	Strain the cream (see note) through a sieve.
3	Put the chocolate, cream and oil into a heatproof bowl set over a pan of simmering water and heat until melted.	4	Transfer to a clean, dry jar and allow to stand until set. The chocolate spread will be the consistency of soft butter.

CHOCOLATE SPREADS

➤ MAKES 1¼ CUPS (300 ML) • PREPARATION: 25 MINUTES • COOKING: 15 MINUTES ◄

CHOCOLATE PRALINE
Infuse 1¼ cups (300 ml) heavy cream (36%) with a split vanilla bean for 15 minutes. Remove the vanilla bean. Melt 10 ounces (300 g) chopped milk chocolate and add the cream. Cool and let thicken slightly, then stir in ⅓ cup (75 ml) crushed pralines.

CHOCOLATE ORANGE GINGER
Infuse 4 lightly crushed cardamom pods and 1 teaspoon (5 ml) finely grated orange zest into 1¼ cups (300 ml) heavy cream (36%). Strain. Melt 10 ounces (300 g) chopped dark or milk chocolate and add the cream. Remove from the heat and stir in ½ cup (125 ml) chopped crystallized ginger.

CHOCOLATE SPREADS

➤MAKES 1¼ CUPS (300 ML) • PREPARATION: 25 MINUTES • COOKING: 15 MINUTES ⬿

RASPBERRY PISTACHIO SWIRL
Infuse 1¼ cups (300 ml) heavy cream (36%) with ⅓ cup (75 ml) finely chopped pistachios; strain. Melt 10 ounces (300 g) grated milk chocolate and add the cream. Cool and let thicken slightly, then stir in ½ cup (125 ml) raspberries and ⅓ cup (75 ml) finely chopped pistachios.

MINT WHITE CHOCOLATE
Infuse 1¼ cups (300 ml) heavy cream (36%) with 6 bruised mint sprigs for 15 minutes. Strain. Melt 10 ounces (300 g) grated dark chocolate and add the cream. Cool and let thicken, then stir in 1¾ ounces (50 g) melted white chocolate.

JELLIES

QUINCE JELLY

❧ MAKES 2 JARS (1 CUP/250 ML) • PREPARATION: 40 MINUTES + DRAINING OVERNIGHT • COOKING: 1½ HOURS ❧

4 pounds (2 kg) quinces, wiped
¼ cup (60 ml) lemon juice
About 4½ cups (1.125 L) granulated sugar,
  warmed

NOTE:
Don't be tempted to hurry the draining
process in step 3 by pushing the fruit
through, as this will result in a cloudy jelly.

1 2
3 4

1	Chop the quinces (do not peel or core) and put into a pan with the lemon juice.	2	Cover with water and bring to a boil. Reduce the heat, cover and simmer for 1 hour, until soft. Mash the quinces until smooth.	
3	Ladle the fruit and liquid into a jelly bag on a stand suspended over a non-metallic bowl. Allow to drain overnight.	4	Put the liquid into a pan, add the sugar and stir over low heat until the sugar has dissolved.	➤

| 5 | Bring to a boil and boil for 25 minutes, until the jelly reaches setting point. Skim any scum from the surface, then remove the pan from the heat. | **TIP**
❋

Jellies can be stored in a cool, dark place for up to a year. |

| 6 | Pour the jelly into clean, dry, sterilized jars and seal. Label and date, then refrigerate after opening. | **NOTE**
❋
Use wet paper towels to wipe the quinces to remove any fuzz. |

POMEGRANATE JELLY

➤ MAKES 1½ JARS (1 CUP/250 ML EACH) • PREPARATION: 20 MINUTES + DRAINING OVERNIGHT • COOKING: 50 MINUTES ➤

6 pounds (3 kg) pomegranates
3 green apples, unpeeled and chopped with
   cores left in

2¼–3⅓ cups (550–825 ml) granulated
   sugar, warmed
¼ cup (60 ml) lemon juice

1 2
3 4

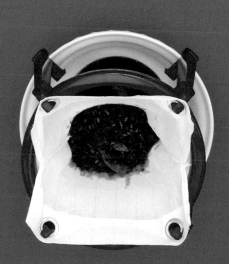

1	Cut the pomegranates in half and juice — you need about 3 cups (750 ml) of juice.	2	Put the pomegranate juice, apples and 1 cup (250 ml) of water in a pan and slowly bring to a boil. Cook until the apple is soft.	
3	Remove from the heat and mash the apple mixture until it is a puree.	4	Ladle the fruit and liquid into a jelly bag on a stand suspended over a non-metallic bowl. Allow to drain overnight.	➤

5	Measure the liquid from the bowl, allowing 2¼ cups (600 ml) of sugar for every 2¼ cups (600 ml) of liquid. Put the liquid into a pan, add the sugar and lemon juice and stir over low heat until the sugar has dissolved. Bring to a boil and boil for 25 minutes, until the jelly reaches setting point. Skim any scum from the surface, then remove from the heat.

VARIATION
❋

Reserve a few seeds before you juice the pomegranate, then put them into the jar before adding the jelly. Stir lightly after adding the jelly to suspend the seeds.

| 6 | Pour the jelly into clean, dry, sterilized jars and seal. Label and date, then refrigerate after opening. | **NOTE**
❋
To remove the juice from the pomegranates, cut them in half and squeeze the juice out with a juicer, as you would for an orange. |

MINT JELLY

⇥ MAKES ABOUT 5 JARS (1 CUP/250 ML EACH) • PREPARATION: 20 MINUTES + 15 MINUTES STANDING & DRAINING OVERNIGHT • COOKING: 40 MINUTES ⇤

3 pounds (1.5 kg) green apples, unpeeled and chopped with cores left in
½ cup (125 ml) finely shredded fresh mint, plus 10 sprigs

4½ cups (1.125 L) granulated sugar, warmed

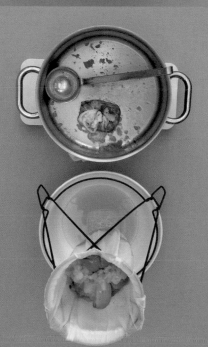

1	Put the apples into a pan and cover with 6 cups (1.5 L) of water. Bring to a boil, reduce the heat and simmer until very soft.	2	Wrap sprigs of mint in a piece of cheesecloth and tie with string, add to the apples and set aside for 15 minutes.
3	Ladle the fruit and liquid into a jelly bag on a stand suspended over a non-metallic bowl. Allow to drain overnight.	4	Put the strained liquid and sugar into a pan and stir over low heat until the sugar has dissolved. ➢

| 5 | Bring to a boil and boil for 25 minutes, until the jelly reaches setting point. Skim any scum from the surface, then remove the pan from the heat. | **VARIATION** ❊

 You can add a pinch of dried mint to the jelly if you don't have any fresh, but don't overdo it — it is much more pungent than the fresh. |

| 6 | Divide the finely shredded mint leaves between clean, dry, sterilized jars. Pour the hot jelly into the jars, stir with a wooden spoon to suspend the mint leaves in the jelly and seal. Label and date, then refrigerate after opening. | **NOTE**
❈

It is important to make sure the mint leaves are dry, or they will not stay suspended in the jelly. |

RED CURRANT JELLY

➤ MAKES 1¼ CUPS (300 ML) • PREPARATION: 20 MINUTES + DRAINING OVERNIGHT • COOKING: 50 MINUTES ➤

3 pounds (1.5kg) red currants
4½ cups (1.125 L) granulated sugar,
    warmed
2 tablespoons (30 ml) lemon juice

1 2
3 4

1	Remove the red currants from their stalks and put the fruit into a pan.	2	Add 1 cup (250 ml) of water and bring to a boil. Reduce the heat and simmer for 15 to 20 minutes, until the fruit is soft and pulpy.	
3	Ladle the fruit and liquid into a jelly bag on a stand suspended over a non-metallic bowl. Allow to drain overnight.	4	Measure the liquid from the bowl, and allow 1 cup (250 ml) of sugar for every 1 cup (250 ml) of liquid.	➤

5
Put the juice, sugar and lemon juice into a pan and stir over low heat until the sugar has dissolved. Bring to a boil and boil for 25 minutes, until the jelly reaches setting point. Skim any scum from the surface, then remove the pan from the heat.

VARIATION
❋

You can use white currants if they are available — this will give you a lovely clear jelly.

| 6 | Pour the hot jelly into clean, dry, sterilized jars and seal. Label and date, then refrigerate after opening. | **TIP**
✻
This jelly will set quickly, so have everything ready to go before you start cooking. |

RED WINE JELLY

➤ MAKES 1¼ CUPS (300ML)• PREPARATION: 20 MINUTES + DRAINING OVERNIGHT • COOKING: 1 HOUR ⥁

2 pounds (1 kg) green apples, cut into
  pieces
2½ cups (625ml) pinot noir

4½ cups (1.125 L) granulated sugar
2 tablespoons (30 ml) lemon juice

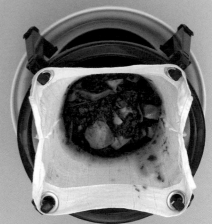

1 2
3 4

1	Put the apples in a pan, add 4 cups (1 L) of water and the wine, cover and simmer for 30 minutes, until the apples are soft and mushy.	2	Ladle the fruit and liquid into a jelly bag on a stand suspended over a non-metallic bowl. Allow to drain overnight.	
3	Measure the liquid from the bowl, allowing 1 cup (250 ml) of sugar for every 1 cup (250 ml) of liquid.	4	Put the liquid, sugar and lemon juice into a pan and stir over low heat until the sugar has dissolved.	➤

| 5 | Bring to a boil and boil for 25 minutes, until the jelly reaches setting point. Skim any scum from the surface, then remove the pan from the heat. | **VARIATION**
❋
You can substitute the pinot with a good-quality Riesling to make white wine jelly. |

		NOTES ❀
6	Pour the hot jelly into clean, dry, sterilized jars and seal. Label and date, then refrigerate after opening.	It is important that you choose a good-quality drinking wine for this recipe, as it will affect the overall taste of the jelly. Do not be tempted to push the fruit through the jelly bag in step 3, or the jelly will be cloudy.

CHILI & KAFFIR LIME JELLY

❖ MAKES 4 JARS (1 CUP/250 ML EACH) • PREPARATION: 30 MINUTES + DRAINING OVERNIGHT • COOKING: 1 HOUR 20 MINUTES ❖

10 kaffir lime leaves, finely shredded
8 large dried red chili peppers
1¾ ounces (50 g) large red chili peppers, chopped

6 stalks lemongrass, chopped
4 pounds (2 kg) green apples, cut into pieces
Zest of 1 lemon, cut into thick strips

4½ cups (1.125 L) granulated sugar, warmed
2 tablespoons (30 ml) lemon juice

1 2
3 4

1	Put the kaffir lime leaves, dried and fresh chilies and lemongrass into a piece of cheese-cloth and tie with string.	2	Put the chopped apples, lemon zest and juice, cheesecloth bag and enough water to cover the apples into a pan and bring to a boil.	
3	Reduce the heat and simmer for 40 minutes, until the apples are very soft and pulpy. Remove and set aside to cool slightly.	4	Pour the apple mixture into a jelly bag suspended over a non-metallic bowl and allow to drain overnight.	➤

5	Measure 1¼ cups (300 ml) of sugar for every 2½ cups (625 ml) of liquid. Put the liquid, sugar and lemon juice into a pan and stir over low heat until the sugar has dissolved. Bring to a boil and boil for 25 minutes, until the jelly reaches setting point. Skim any scum from the surface, then remove the pan from the heat.	**VARIATION**
		If you can't find fresh or frozen kaffir lime leaves, omit them and make a chili jelly instead.

		NOTES
6	Pour the hot jelly into clean, dry, sterilized jars and seal. Label and date, then refrigerate after opening.	Do not be tempted to push the fruit through the jelly bag at step 4, or the jelly will be cloudy. You will get the best flavor from this jelly if you find fresh kaffir lime leaves — frozen will also give a good flavor, but you will struggle to achieve the same quality using dried ones.

MARMALADES

4

LIME & GINGER MARMALADE

⇾ MAKES 4 JARS (1 CUP/250 ML EACH) • PREPARATION: 30 MINUTES + SOAKING OVERNIGHT • COOKING: 1 HOUR 20 MINUTES ⇽

2 pounds (1 kg) limes
1¼ cups (30 ml) granulated sugar
8 ounces (250 g) crystallized ginger

1 2
3 4

1	Cut the limes in half, then slice thinly.	2	Put the lime slices in a non-metallic bowl and add 8 cups (2 L) of water. Cover and leave overnight.	
3	Put the lime mixture in a pan, cover and cook for 50 minutes. Add the sugar and ginger and stir over low heat until the sugar has dissolved.	4	Boil for 20 minutes, until setting point is reached.	➤

5	Remove from the heat and skim the scum from the surface. Allow to stand for 10 minutes. Spoon the marmalade into warm, dry, sterilized jars, then seal and process in a boiling water canner for 10 minutes.	**TIP** ❉ Stir the marmalade twice while it is boiling in step 4.	

6	Label and date, then refrigerate the marmalade after opening.	**NOTES** ※ Scrub the limes under warm running water with a soft bristle brush to remove any dirt before using. When the marmalade falls from a tilted wooden spoon in thick sheets without dripping, it is ready to be tested, to see if the mixture has reached setting point.

GRAPEFRUIT MARMALADE

❧ MAKES 8 JARS (1 CUP/250 ML EACH) • PREPARATION: 5 MINUTES + SOAKING OVERNIGHT • COOKING: 30 MINUTES ❧

2 pounds (1 kg) pink grapefruit, scrubbed
⅓ cup (75 ml) lemon juice
9 cups (2.25 L) granulated sugar, warmed

1 2
3 4

1	Cut the grapefruit in half, then into eighths, then cut into ¼-inch (0.5 cm) thick slices. Discard the seeds.	2	Put the grapefruit in a non-metallic bowl along with the lemon juice and 8 cups (2 L) of water. Leave overnight.
3	Put the grapefruit, reserved liquid and sugar into a pan and stir over low heat to dissolve the sugar. Boil for 20 minutes, until setting point.	4	Allow to stand for 10 minutes, then skim to disperse any scum. Spoon into dry, sterilized jars, seal and process. Chill after opening.

THREE-FRUIT JELLY MARMALADE

❧ MAKES 3 TO 4 JARS (1 CUP/250 ML EACH) • PREPARATION: 20 MINUTES + 3 HOURS DRAINING • COOKING: 40 MINUTES ❧

1 pound (500 g) limes, scrubbed
1 pound (500 g) lemons, scrubbed
1 pound (500 g) oranges, scrubbed

6¾ cups (1.675 L) granulated sugar, warmed
⅓ cup (75 ml) lemon juice

1 2
3 4

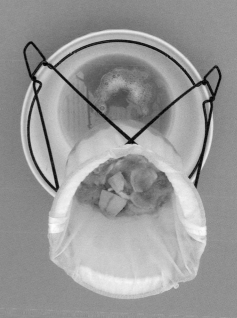

1	Remove the rind from each citrus fruit and discard half. Shred half of the remaining rind and put the other half into cheesecloth and tie with string.	2	Cut the fruit in half, then squeeze the juice, remove the seeds and set aside. Chop the flesh, leaving the pith on.	
3	Put the fruit, juice, the cheesecloth bag and 4 cups (1 L) of water into a pan, cover with a lid and simmer for 30 minutes.	4	Pour the fruit and juices into a clean jelly bag and leave for 3 hours to drain.	➤

5	Measure the drained liquid, transfer to a clean pan and add 1 cup (250 ml) of sugar for every 1 cup (250 ml) of liquid. Add the lemon juice, sugar and shredded rind and stir over low heat to dissolve the sugar. Bring to a boil and cook for 10 minutes, stirring twice, until the mixture reaches setting point.	**VARIATION** ❈ You can also make this marmalade using just one citrus fruit, if you prefer.

6	Remove from the heat and allow to stand for 10 minutes, then skim the surface to remove any scum. Spoon the marmalade into warm, dry, sterilized jars, then seal and process in a boiling water canner for 10 minutes. Label and date, and refrigerate after opening.

NOTES
❋

When the marmalade falls from a tilted wooden spoon in thick sheets without dripping, it is ready to test if the mixture has reached setting point.

The amount of rind you will need will depend on the size of the jars you use — make sure to remove as much of the pith as you can and cut it as thinly as possible.

CLEMENTINE MARMALADE

MAKES 4 JARS (1 CUP/250 ML EACH) • PREPARATION: 20 MINUTES + SOAKING OVERNIGHT • COOKING: 1½ HOURS

1 pound (1 kg) seedless clementines
4 sprigs rosemary

6¾ cups (1.675 L) granulated sugar,
   warmed
2 tablespoons (30 ml) lemon juice

1 2
3 4

1	Scrub the clementines and dry thoroughly with a tea towel.	2	Thinly slice the clementines.	
3	Put the clementines, rosemary and 7 cups (1.75 L) of water into a pan and boil for 30 minutes. Remove from the heat, cover and leave overnight.	4	Next day, bring the mixture to a boil, add the sugar and lemon juice and cook until dissolved. Boil for 45–60 minutes, until setting point. Remove rosemary.	➤

		TIP
5	Allow the marmalade to stand for 10 minutes. Spoon into warm, dry, sterilized jars, then seal and process in a boiling water canner for 10 minutes. Label and date, and chill after opening.	Once opened, this marmalade should be used within a year.

| 6 | Serve this marmalade on toast or bagels for breakfast. | **NOTE** ❈

When the marmalade falls from a tilted wooden spoon in thick sheets without dripping, it is ready to be tested, to see if the mixture has reached setting point. |

KUMQUAT MARMALADE

❖ MAKES 6 JARS (1 CUP/250 ML EACH) • PREPARATION: 40 MINUTES + SOAKING OVERNIGHT • COOKING: 1 HOUR ❖

2 pounds (1 kg) kumquats
4½ cups (1.125 L) granulated sugar,
    warmed

¼ cup (60ml) lemon juice
¼ cup (60ml) brandy

1	Cut the kumquats into quarters and remove and reserve the seeds.	2	Put the seeds into a piece of cheesecloth and tie with string.	3	Put the fruit, 4 cups (1 L) of water and cheesecloth bag in pan. Boil for 30 minutes.
4	Put the fruit in their liquid and the cheesecloth bag in a non-metallic bowl, cover and leave overnight.	5	Put mixture into a pan, add sugar and lemon juice, stir over low heat to dissolve sugar, then boil until set.	6	Remove cheesecloth bag, let stand for 10 minutes, then stir in the brandy. Spoon into sterilized jars, seal, process and label.

LEMON MARMALADE

❧ MAKES 6 JARS (1 CUP/250 ML EACH) • PREPARATION: 40 MINUTES + SOAKING OVERNIGHT • COOKING: 1½ HOURS ❧

1 pound (500g) lemons, scrubbed, halved,
   seeded and thinly sliced
6¾ cups (1.675 L) granulated sugar,
   warmed

NOTE:
When removing the seeds from the
lemons, make sure you remove any white
membrane.

1	Put the lemon slices into a pan with 7 cups (1.75 L) of water and boil for 30 minutes. Cover and leave overnight.	2	Next day, bring the lemon mixture to a boil, add the sugar and stir until it has dissolved. Boil for 45–60 minutes, until setting point.
3	Remove from the heat, put a little marmalade onto a frozen plate, and if a skin forms when you push your finger through it, it is ready.	4	Allow to stand for 10 minutes, then spoon the marmalade into warm, dry, sterilized jars, seal and process. Label and date, then chill after opening.

MUSTARDS

5

TARRAGON MUSTARD

✦ MAKES 1 CUP (250 ML) • PREPARATION: 10 MINUTES + STANDING 15 MINUTES + OVERNIGHT • COOKING: NONE ✦

½ cup (125 ml) yellow mustard seeds
½ cup (125 ml) tarragon vinegar
2 teaspoons (10 ml) lemon juice
½ teaspoon (2 ml) salt

2 shallots, finely chopped
1½ tablespoons (22 ml) chopped fresh
 tarragon

NOTE:
This mustard will keep for 3 months
unopened.

1 2
3 4

1	Soak the mustard seeds in 2 tablespoons (30 ml) of water for 15 minutes. Add vinegar, lemon juice, salt and shallots, cover and leave overnight.	2	The next day, transfer the mixture to a blender or food processor and process until smooth.
3	Stir in the chopped tarragon. Spoon the mustard into a clean, warm and dry jar, filling right to the top of the jar.	4	Seal and store for 2 to 4 weeks for the flavors to develop, then refrigerate after opening.

MAPLE WHOLE-GRAIN MUSTARD

➤ MAKES 3 CUPS (750 ML) • PREPARATION: 15 MINUTES + STANDING OVERNIGHT • COOKING: NONE ➤

3 tablespoons (45 ml) black mustard seeds
½ cup (125 ml) yellow mustards seeds
½ cup (125 ml) white balsamic vinegar

½ teaspoon (2 ml) sea salt
2 teaspoons (10 ml) lemon juice
1 tablespoon (15 ml) maple syrup

1	Put the mustard seeds and 2 tablespoons (30 ml) of water in a non-metallic bowl. Cover and leave overnight.	2	The next day, transfer three-quarters of the mixture to a blender or food processor and add the vinegar, salt, lemon juice and maple syrup.
3	Process the mustard mixture until roughly crushed.	4	Transfer to a bowl and stir in the remaining seeds. Spoon into a warm, dry jar. Seal and store for 2 to 4 weeks. Chill after opening.

PINK PEPPER & CAPER MUSTARD

❧ MAKES 1¼ CUPS (300 ML) • PREPARATION: 10 MINUTES + STANDING 20 MINUTES + OVERNIGHT • COOKING: NONE ❧

¾ cups (175 ml) yellow mustard seeds
½ cup (125 ml) white wine vinegar
1 teaspoon (5 ml) brown sugar

2 tablespoons (30 ml) chopped drained
    capers
1 teaspoon (5 ml) crushed pink peppercorns
½ teaspoon (2 ml) salt

1 2
3 4

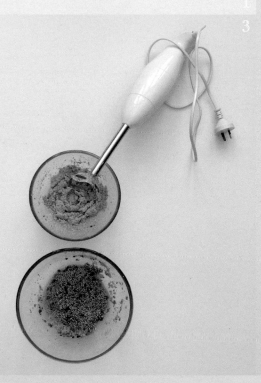

1	Put the mustards seeds and 2 tablespoons (30 ml) of water in a non-metallic bowl and leave for 20 minutes.	2	Add the vinegar, brown sugar, capers and peppercorns, cover and leave overnight.	
3	The next day, transfer half of the mixture to a food processor, or use a handheld blender or a mortar and pestle, and blitz until smooth.	4	Add the ground mixture to the remaining seeds and peppercorns and mix well. Stir in the salt.	➤

5	Spoon the mustard into a clean, warm, dry jar, filling it right to the top of the jar.	**VARIATIONS** ❋ Substitute the chopped capers with finely chopped green or black pitted olives, if you like.

| 6 | Seal and store for 2 to 4 weeks, then refrigerate after opening. | **NOTE** ❈

You can use half mustard powder and yellow mustard seeds to make this recipe if you don't have a blender or mortar and pestle. |

GARLIC & PARSLEY MUSTARD

❖ MAKES 2 CUPS (500 ML) • PREPARATION: 20 MINUTES + STANDING OVERNIGHT • COOKING: 15 MINUTES ❖

¾ cups (175 ml) yellow mustard seeds
1 tablespoon (15 ml) dry mustard powder
1 cup (250 ml) white wine vinegar
2 cloves garlic, cut in half

1 teaspoon (5 ml) superfine sugar
2 tablespoons (30 ml) chopped parsley
2 teaspoons (10 ml) lemon juice
½ teaspoon (2 ml) sea salt

NOTE:
In step 2, stir the vinegar and sugar mixture over low heat until the sugar has dissolved. It is ready when the garlic is soft.

1 2
3 4

1	Put the mustard seeds, mustard powder and ½ cup (125 ml) of water in a non-metallic bowl, cover and leave overnight.	2	Next day, heat the vinegar, garlic and sugar. When sugar has dissolved, boil, then reduce heat and simmer for 10 minutes. Cool slightly.
3	Put the mustard mixture and the garlic and vinegar mixture into a food processor, add the lemon juice and salt and process until smooth.	4	Spoon the mustard into a clean, warm, dry jar, filling it to the top of the jar. Seal and store for 2 to 4 weeks, then refrigerate after opening.

SPICED FRENCH MUSTARD

❖ MAKES 1¼ CUPS (300 ML) • PREPARATION: 20 MINUTES + STANDING OVERNIGHT • COOKING: 15 MINUTES ❖

¼ cup (60 ml) brown mustard seeds
2 tablespoons (30 ml) dry mustard powder
¼ cup (60 ml) cider vinegar

2 tablespoons (30 ml) brown sugar
½ teaspoon (2 ml) ground cinnamon
¼ teaspoon (1 ml) ground allspice

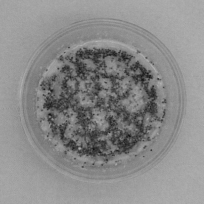

1 2
3 4

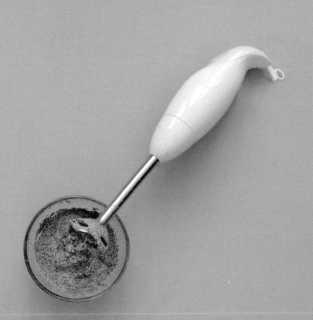

1	Put the mustard seeds, mustard powder and 3 tablespoons (45 ml) of water in a non-metallic bowl. Cover and leave overnight.	2	Next day, put the remaining ingredients into a pan and stir over low heat until sugar dissolves. Boil, reduce the heat and simmer until thick.
3	Pour the mustard seed mixture and the vinegar mixture into a food processor and blitz until smooth, or use a handheld blender.	4	Spoon the mustard into a clean, warm, dry jar, filling it to the top of the jar. Seal and store for 2 to 4 weeks, then refrigerate after opening.

HONEY MUSTARD

❖ MAKES ⅔ CUPS (150 ML) • PREPARATION: 20 MINUTES • COOKING: 20 MINUTES ❖

½ cup (125 ml) yellow mustard seeds
2 tablespoons (30 ml) liquid honey
½ cup (125 ml) packed brown sugar

2 teaspoons (10 ml) cider vinegar
1 tablespoon (15 ml) canola oil

NOTE:
You can also make this mustard using mustard powder.

1 2
3 4

1	Put the mustard seeds in a mortar and pound with a pestle to form a fine powder. Transfer to a small pan.	2	Add 3 tablespoons (45 ml) of water, or enough to form a paste.
3	Add the honey, brown sugar, vinegar and oil and stir over low heat until the sugar dissolves and the mustard is smooth.	4	Spoon into clean, warm, dry jars and leave for 2 weeks, for the flavors to develop.

CHUTNEYS & RELISHES

6

ONION & THYME MARMALADE

❖ MAKES 6 JARS (1 CUP/250 ML EACH) • PREPARATION: 30 MINUTES • COOKING: 1½ HOURS ❖

½ cup (125 ml) olive oil
4 pounds (2 kg) onions, thinly sliced
1 teaspoon (5 ml) sea salt
2 bay leaves
1 cinnamon stick

1 tablespoon (15 ml) fresh thyme leaves
½ cup (125 ml) balsamic vinegar
1 cup (250 ml) malt vinegar
2 cups (500 ml) packed brown sugar

1 2
3 4

1	Heat the oil in a large pan, add the onions and cook over medium heat for 40 minutes, until soft and golden.	2	Add the salt, bay leaves, cinnamon, thyme, vinegars and brown sugar and stir over low heat until the sugar has dissolved.
3	Bring to a boil, reduce the heat and simmer for 30 minutes, until thick and syrupy. Remove the bay leaves and cinnamon stick.	4	Spoon the onion marmalade into dry, sterilized jars. Seal and process for 10 minutes. Label and date, then refrigerate after opening.

PICCALILLI

❖ MAKES 6 JARS (1 CUP/250 ML) • PREPARATION: 20 MINUTES + STANDING OVERNIGHT • COOKING: 10 MINUTES ❖

1 pound (500 g) cauliflower, cut into florets
1 cucumber, chopped
7 ounces (200 g) green beans, cut into
    ¾-inch pieces (about 2 cups/500 ml)
1 onion, chopped
2 carrots, chopped

⅓ cup (75 ml) salt
1 cup (250 ml) demerara sugar
1 teaspoon (5 ml) black mustard seeds
2 teaspoons (10 ml) ground turmeric
1 teaspoon (5 ml) ground ginger
2 small dried red chili peppers

4 cups (1 L) white wine vinegar
⅓ cup (75 ml) all-purpose flour
2 tablespoons (30 ml) mustard powder

1 2
3 4

1	Put the vegetables and salt in a non-metallic bowl and mix. Cover the vegetables with a plate and allow to stand overnight.	2	The next day, rinse the vegetables under cold running water and drain well.	
3	Put the vegetables, sugar, spices and three-quarters of the vinegar in a pan and stir over low heat to dissolve sugar. Boil, then simmer for 5 minutes.	4	Blend the flour with the mustard and remaining vinegar.	➤

| 5 | Add the flour mixture to the vegetables and cook, stirring, until the mixture boils and thickens. | **TIP**
❈
You can use Dijon, grainy or hot English mustard instead of mustard powder. The hot English mustard will give you a fiery piccalilli. |

| 6 | Spoon the piccalilli into dry, sterilized jars, then seal and process in a boiling water canner for 10 minutes. Label and date. Leave for 1 month, then chill after opening. | **NOTE**
❋
The flavor of the piccalilli will mellow, so it is best if you allow it to stand for a couple of weeks before serving. |

RED PEPPER & CHILI CHUTNEY

❧ MAKES 6 JARS (1 CUP/250 ML) • PREPARATION: 20 MINUTES • COOKING: 1¾ HOURS + COOLING TIME ❦

2 pounds (1 kg) ripe tomatoes, preferably
 plum (Roma), cut in half
2 pounds (1 kg) red peppers
1 head garlic
2 red onions

2 large fresh red chilies
1½ cups (375 ml) packed brown sugar
1½ cups (375 ml) red wine vinegar
¼ cup (60 ml) lemon juice

1 2
3 4

1	Preheat the oven to 350°F (180°C). Roast the tomatoes, peppers, garlic, onions and chilies for 1 hour. Cool slightly.	2	Peel the garlic, roughly chop the tomatoes, peppers, garlic, onions and chilies (remove the seeds, if you like) and put in a pan.
3	Add the brown sugar, vinegar and lemon juice and stir over low heat to dissolve the sugar. Bring to a boil, reduce the heat and cook until thick.	4	Spoon the chutney into dry, sterilized jars, then seal and process for 15 minutes. Label and date. Leave for 1 month, then chill after opening.

SPICY BEET RELISH

➤ MAKES 4 JARS (1 CUP/250 ML EACH) • PREPARATION: 30 MINUTES • COOKING: 50 MINUTES ◄

2 pounds (1 kg) fresh beets
10 ounces (300 g) green apples, peeled, cored and grated
1 onion, chopped

2 cloves garlic, chopped
¾ cup (175 ml) raisins
1 teaspoon (5 ml) ground allspice

2 tablespoons (30 ml) grated fresh horseradish
1⅔ cups (400 ml) malt vinegar
1 cup (250 ml) packed brown sugar

1 2
3 4

1	Peel and coarsely grate the beets.	2	Put the beets, apples, onion, garlic and 4 cups (1 L) of water in a pan and cook for 20 minutes, until the apples are soft.
3	Add the raisins, allspice, horseradish, vinegar and brown sugar and stir over low heat to dissolve the sugar. Boil for 30 minutes, until thick.	4	Spoon into dry, sterilized jars and seal with vinegar-proof lids. Label and date. Leave for 1 month, and chill after opening.

SPICED FRUIT CHUTNEY

❧ MAKES 6 JARS (1 CUP/250 ML EACH) • PREPARATION: 30 MINUTES • COOKING: 1¾ HOURS ❧

1¾ ounces (50 g) fresh ginger, sliced
2 small dried chili peppers
6 whole cloves
1 teaspoon (5 ml) fennel seeds
1 cinnamon stick

1 pound (500 g) tomatoes, chopped
2 pounds (1 kg) green apples, peeled, cored
  and diced
1 pound (500 g) onions, chopped
1½ cups (375 ml) raisins

1½ cups (375 ml) dried apricots, chopped
2 cups (500 ml) packed brown sugar
2 cups (500 ml) apple cider vinegar

1	Put the spices into a spice basket or tea ball.	2	Put the spice basket, tomatoes, apples, onions, raisins, apricots, brown sugar and vinegar into a pan and stir over low heat to dissolve the sugar.
3	Simmer, uncovered, for 1 to 1½ hours. Remove the spice basket.	4	Spoon into dry, sterilized jars and seal with vinegar-proof lids. Label and date. Leave for 1 month, and chill after opening.

FIG, PEAR & PEPPER CHUTNEY

➺ MAKES 7 JARS (1 CUP/250 ML EACH) • PREPARATION: 20 MINUTES • COOKING: 45 MINUTES

1 teaspoon (5 ml) Szechuan pepper
1 teaspoon (5 ml) white pepper
3 whole star anise
1 cinnamon stick
Zest of 1 orange

3 pounds (1.5 kg) green apples, peeled, cored and roughly chopped
1 pound (500 g) pears, peeled, cored and roughly chopped
10 ounces (300 g) dried figs, chopped

1 pound (500 g) small red shallots, peeled and chopped
2½ cups (625 ml) rice vinegar
2 cups (500 ml) packed brown sugar

1 2
3 4

1	Roast both peppers in a dry frying pan until fragrant.	2	Put the peppers, star anise, cinnamon stick and orange zest onto a piece of cheesecloth and tie with string.
3	Put fruit, shallots, spice bag, vinegar and brown sugar into a pan and stir over low heat to dissolve the sugar. Boil, then simmer for 30–40 minutes.	4	Remove the spice bag. Spoon into warm, dry, sterilized jars and seal with vinegar-proof lids. Leave for a few months, and chill after opening.

CHILI PASTE

➤ MAKES 2 CUPS (500 ML) • PREPARATION: 1 HOUR • COOKING: 5½ HOURS ➤

3 cups (750 ml) vegetable oil
12 large fresh red chili peppers
2 heads garlic, peeled and sliced
1 pound (500 g) small red shallots, sliced
3½ ounces (100 g) dried shrimp

2 teaspoons (10 ml) shrimp paste (optional)
½ cup (125 ml) grated palm sugar or brown
  sugar
1½ tablespoons (22 ml) tamarind puree

1 2
3 4

1	Heat oil for deep-frying and fry the chilies, garlic, shallots and shrimp in batches until crisp and golden. Drain on paper towels.	2	Process the chili mixture in a food processor until smooth.
3	Heat ⅓ cup (75 ml) of the vegetable oil, add the chili paste, shrimp paste and sugar and cook gently for 4 hours, until deep red.	4	Add the tamarind puree and cook for 1 hour longer. Spoon into dry, sterilized jars and seal with vinegar-proof lids. Leave for a few months.

PEAR & CHILI CHUTNEY

❧ MAKES 4 JARS (1 CUP/250 ML EACH) • PREPARATION: 30 MINUTES • COOKING: 50 MINUTES ❧

3 pounds (1.5 kg) pears, peeled, cored and
   chopped
1 bunch green onions, chopped
3 tablespoons (45 ml) fresh grated ginger

2 teaspoons (10 ml) pickling spice
2 tablespoons (30 ml) chopped cilantro root
2 large green fresh chili peppers, chopped
1 cup (250 ml) white vinegar

2 tablespoons (30 ml) fish sauce
1 cup (250 ml) packed brown sugar
1 cup (250 ml) chopped fresh cilantro
2 tablespoons (30 ml) lime juice

1 2
3 4

1	Put the pears, onions, ginger, spice, cilantro roots, chilies, vinegar, fish sauce and brown sugar in a pan and stir over low heat to dissolve the sugar.	2	Bring to a boil, then reduce the heat and simmer, uncovered, for 30 to 40 minutes, until thick and pulpy.
3	Stir in the chopped cilantro and lime juice and mix to combine.	4	Spoon the chutney into dry, sterilized jars, seal with vinegar-proof lids and process. This chutney can be eaten immediately.

ASIAN PLUM SAUCE

❧ MAKES 6 JARS (1 CUP/250 ML EACH) • PREPARATION: 20 MINUTES • COOKING: 1 HOUR ❧

2 large dried red chili peppers
1 cinnamon stick
3 whole star anise
3 garlic cloves, chopped

2 tablespoons (30 ml) grated fresh ginger
1 onion, chopped
1 green apple, peeled, cored and chopped
3 pounds (1.5 kg) plums, pitted and
    chopped

2 cups (500 ml) packed brown sugar
1½ cups (375 ml) rice vinegar
¼ cup (60 ml) soy sauce

1 2
3 4

1	Put chilies and spices into a piece of cheesecloth and tie with string. Process the garlic, ginger and onion in a food processor until smooth.	2	Transfer the garlic mixture to a pan with the remaining ingredients and stir over low heat until the brown sugar has dissolved.	
3	Bring to a boil, then reduce the heat and cook for 40 minutes, until thick and pulpy. Remove and discard the cheesecloth bag.	4	Remove the pan from the heat and, using a handheld blender, blitz until smooth.	➤

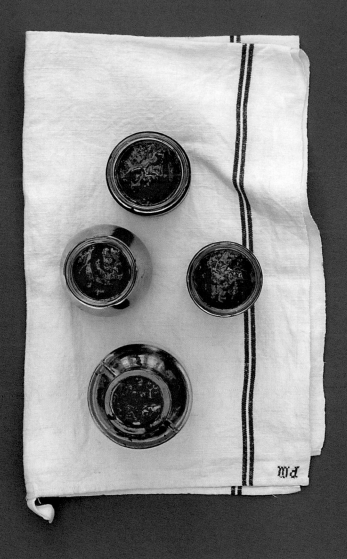

| 5 | Spoon the relish into dry, sterilized jars, then seal with vinegar-proof lids and process in a boiling water canner for 10 minutes. Label and date. | **TIP**
❋
Serve this sauce as part of a Chinese meal. It is especially good with crispy Peking duck pancakes. |

6	Leave the sauce for a few months, then refrigerate after opening.	**NOTE** ✳ Once opened, use this sauce within 6 weeks.

SPICED SQUASH CHUTNEY

❧ MAKES 5 JARS (1 CUP/250 ML EACH) • PREPARATION: 30 MINUTES • COOKING: 40 MINUTES ❧

2 tablespoons (30 ml) grated fresh ginger
4 cloves garlic
3 tablespoons (45 ml) vegetable oil
2 onions, chopped
1 teaspoon (5 ml) fennel seeds

1 teaspoon (5 ml) black mustard seeds
1 teaspoon (5 ml) ground turmeric
1 teaspoon (5 ml) ground cinnamon
1 teaspoon (5 ml) garam masala
1 teaspoon (5 ml) salt

3 dried chili peppers
2 pounds (1 kg) butternut squash, peeled,
   seeded and cut into chunks
1 cup (250 ml) malt vinegar
1 cup (250 ml) packed brown sugar

1 2
3 4

1	Put the ginger and garlic into a food processor and blitz to form a smooth paste.	2	Heat the oil in a pan, add the onion and cook for 10 minutes, until soft. Add the ginger paste and spices and cook for 2 minutes.
3	Add the squash, vinegar and brown sugar and stir over low heat until the sugar has dissolved. Boil, reduce the heat and simmer until thick.	4	Spoon the chutney into dry, sterilized jars, then seal with vinegar-proof lids and process. This chutney can be eaten immediately.

LAVOSH

❧ MAKES 8 PIECES • PREPARATION: 20 MINUTES • COOKING: 10 TO 15 MINUTES ❧

2½ cups (625 ml) all-purpose flour
1 teaspoon (5 ml) superfine sugar
1 teaspoon (5 ml) salt
1 egg white
2 tablespoons (30 ml) olive oil

TOPPING
1 egg white
Sea salt, to taste
4 sprigs rosemary

1 2
3 4

1	Preheat oven to 400°F (200°C). Line 2 to 3 baking sheets with parchment paper. Sift the flour into a bowl and stir in the sugar and salt.	2	Add the egg white, olive oil and ⅔ cup (150 ml) of water and mix to form a soft dough.	
3	Turn the dough out onto a lightly floured surface and knead gently to form a soft ball.	4	Divide the dough into 8 equal-sized pieces and roll each piece into a long tongue shape.	➤

5	Brush with egg white and sprinkle with sea salt and rosemary (or your choice of topping).

VARIATIONS
❋

Make large tongues of lavosh to serve with an antipasto platter. Try adding the rosemary to the dry ingredients so the flavor is more pronounced.

6	Place the lavosh onto the prepared baking sheets and bake for 10 to 15 minutes, until crisp and golden. Serve with cheese and chutney. Allow guests to break their lavosh into pieces.	**NOTE** ❋ The lavosh will keep for up to 1 week if kept in an airtight container.

INDIAN MANGO CHUTNEY

✦ MAKES 4 JARS (1 CUP/250 ML EACH) • PREPARATION: 20 MINUTES • COOKING: 50 MINUTES ✦

5 pounds (2.5 kg) green mangoes (not ripe)
1 onion, chopped
1 tablespoon (15 ml) grated fresh ginger
⅔ cup (150 ml) white vinegar

½ cup (125 ml) packed brown sugar
½ teaspoon (2 ml) garam masala
½ teaspoon (2 ml) chili powder

NOTE:
The chutney is ready when you can drag your wooden spoon through the center of the mixture and it holds a line.

1 2
3 4

1	Peel the mangoes, remove the pits and chop the flesh.	2	Put the mangoes, onion, ginger, vinegar, brown sugar, garam masala and chili powder into a pan and cook over low heat to dissolve the sugar.
3	Boil, then reduce the heat and simmer for 40 minutes, checking regularly that the mixture is not catching on the bottom of the pan.	4	Spoon into dry, sterilized jars, and seal with vinegar-proof lids. Label and date. Leave for a few months, then chill after opening.

TOMATO & DATE CHUTNEY

❧ MAKES ABOUT 5½ JARS (1 CUP/250 ML EACH) • PREPARATION: 20 MINUTES • COOKING: 1 HOUR ❧

3 large dried red chili peppers
6 fresh curry leaves
4 slices fresh ginger
3 pounds (1.5 kg) tomatoes, chopped

1 pound (500 g) onions, chopped
8 ounces (250 g) pitted dates, chopped
1 teaspoon (5 ml) black mustard seeds

⅔ cup (150 ml) white vinegar
1 cup (250 ml) packed brown sugar
½ cup (125 ml) tamarind puree

1	Put the chilies, curry leaves and ginger into a piece of cheesecloth and tie with string.	2	Put the tomatoes, onions, dates, mustard seeds, vinegar, brown sugar and cheesecloth bag into a pan and cook over low heat to dissolve the sugar.
3	Boil, then reduce the heat and simmer for 40 minutes, checking regularly that the mixture is not sticking to the bottom of the pan.	4	Remove the cheesecloth bag and stir in the tamarind puree. Return to a boil and cook for 5 minutes. ➤

5	Spoon the chutney into warm, dry, sterilized jars and seal with vinegar-proof lids. Label and date.	**TIP** When the chutney is spooned into the jars, push the mixture down to remove any air.

6	Leave the chutney for a few months, then chill after opening.	**NOTE** ❋ The chutney is ready when you can drag a wooden spoon through the center of the mixture and it holds a line.

INDIAN EGGPLANT PICKLE

❖ MAKES ABOUT 4 JARS (1 CUP/250 ML EACH) • PREPARATION: 30 MINUTES + 30 MINUTES STANDING • COOKING: 50 MINUTES ❖

2 large eggplants
3 tablespoons (45 ml) salt
4 cloves garlic, peeled
2 tablespoons (30 ml) grated fresh ginger
4 large fresh green chili peppers

1 cup (250 ml) mustard or peanut oil
1 teaspoon (5 ml) ground turmeric
2 teaspoons (10 ml) chili powder
1 teaspoon (5 ml) ground cumin
1 teaspoon (5 ml) fenugreek seeds

6 curry leaves
1 cup (250 ml) malt vinegar
2 tablespoons (30 ml) grated palm sugar or
   brown sugar

1 2
3 4

1	Remove the stems from the eggplants, cut the flesh into cubes, place in a colander and sprinkle with salt. Leave for 30 minutes.	2	Pound with a mortar and pestle or process the garlic, ginger and chilies in a food processor to form a smooth paste.	
3	Heat the oil in a pan, add the turmeric, chili powder, cumin and fenugreek and cook, stirring, for 5 minutes.	4	Add the chili paste and curry leaves and cook for 10 minutes, until the oil rises to the surface.	➤

5	Add the unrinsed eggplant to the pan and cook for 10 minutes. Add the vinegar and brown sugar and cook for a further 15 to 20 minutes, until the eggplant is soft.	**TIP** ❋ When the pickle is spooned into the jars, push the mixture down to remove any air.

6	Spoon the pickle into dry, sterilized jars and seal with vinegar-proof lids. Allow to rest, then refrigerate after opening.	**NOTE** ❊ Once opened, use this pickle within 6 weeks.

INDIAN LIME PICKLE

➤ MAKES 2 JARS (4 CUPS/1 L EACH) • PREPARATION: 30 MINUTES + 1 WEEK STANDING • COOKING: 5 MINUTES ◄

14 limes
1 cup (250 ml) salt
¼ cup (60 ml) lime juice
2 tablespoons (30 ml) vegetable oil

1 teaspoon (5 ml) fenugreek seeds
1 teaspoon (5 ml) black mustard seeds
2 teaspoons (10 ml) ground turmeric
1 teaspoon (5 ml) asafetida powder

½ cup (125 ml) chili powder or powdered
  medium & hot chili peppers or hot paprika
2 tablespoons (30 ml) granulated sugar

1 2
3 4

1	Wash and thoroughly dry the limes.	2	Cut the limes in half, then into quarters and then cut each quarter in half.	
3	Put the lime pieces in a bowl, add the salt and lime juice and mix to coat the limes in the salt.	4	Pack the limes into a clean, dry 4-cup (1 L) glass jar. Seal and leave at room temperature for 1 week.	➤

5 6
7 8

5	After 1 week, heat the oil in a small pan, add the fenugreek and black mustard seeds and cook for 1 minute, until golden.	6	Transfer the seeds to a mortar and pestle or spice grinder, add the turmeric and asafetida and grind until powdery.
7	Put the spice mixture, chili powder, sugar and marinated limes into a clean, dry non-metallic bowl and mix to combine.	8	Spoon the mixture back into two 4-cup (1 L) jars (or as necessary), seal and store for 2 weeks at room temperature in a sunny place.

9	After 2 weeks, the pickle can be used. Chill in the refrigerator after opening and use within 6 weeks.	**TIP** ❋ This pickle is great served with pappadams as an appetizer before an Indian meal.

SHALLOT & FENNEL CONFIT

➤ MAKES 3 JARS (1 CUP/250 ML EACH) • PREPARATION: 30 MINUTES • COOKING: 1 HOUR ◄

2 pounds (1 kg) fennel, sliced
3 tablespoons (45 ml) olive oil
1 pound (500 g) long red (French) shallots,
   chopped

4 cloves garlic, chopped
1 teaspoon (5 ml) fennel seeds
1 teaspoon (5 ml) ground cinnamon
1 teaspoon (5 ml) ground cumin

½ cup (125 ml) white wine
1 cup (250 ml) malt vinegar
1 cup (250 ml) packed brown sugar

1	Put the fennel in a pan, add 2 cups (500 ml) water and bring to a boil. Simmer until soft.	2	Heat the oil in another pan, add the shallots and cook for 20 minutes, until soft.	3	Drain the fennel and add to the shallots. Cook until it starts to brown.
4	Add the garlic and spices and cook for 3 minutes, until fragrant.	5	Stir in the wine, vinegar and brown sugar. Boil for 30 minutes, until thick and pulpy.	6	Spoon into dry, sterilized jars and seal with vinegar-proof lids. Allow to rest, then chill after opening.

GREEN TOMATO CHUTNEY

❧ MAKES 4 JARS (1 CUP/250 ML EACH) • PREPARATION: 20 MINUTES • COOKING: 40 MINUTES ❧

2 fresh red chili peppers, cut in half
2 tablespoons (30 ml) grated fresh ginger
1 cinnamon stick
3 pounds (1.5 kg) green tomatoes

1 pound (500 g) green apples
2 onions, chopped
1 cup (250 ml) packed light brown sugar
2 cups (500 ml) malt or cider vinegar

1 teaspoon (5 ml) celery seeds
1 teaspoon (5 ml) cumin seeds
1 teaspoon (5 ml) coriander seeds
1 teaspoon (5 ml) yellow mustard seeds

1 2
3 4

1	Put the chilies, ginger and cinnamon stick into a piece of cheesecloth and tie with string.	2	Place the tomatoes, apples, onions, brown sugar, vinegar, spices and cheesecloth bag into a pan and stir over low heat to dissolve the sugar.
3	Bring to a boil and cook for 30 minutes, until the chutney is thick and pulpy. Remove and discard the cheesecloth bag.	4	Spoon into dry, sterilized jars and seal with vinegar-proof lids. Label and date. Allow to rest, then chill after opening.

ROASTED TOMATO KETCHUP

➤ MAKES 4 JARS (1 CUP/250 ML EACH) • PREPARATION: 30 MINUTES • COOKING: 1¼ HOURS ➤

4 pounds (2 kg) ripe tomatoes
10 ounces (300 g) onions (about 2 medium),
   chopped
4 cloves garlic
3 sprigs thyme

3 sprigs rosemary
2 tablespoons (30 ml) olive oil
Salt and black pepper, to taste
¼ cup (60 ml) malt vinegar
⅓ cup (75 ml) packed brown sugar

1 teaspoon (5 ml) ground ginger
1 teaspoon (5 ml) fennel seeds
1 teaspoon (5 ml) mustard powder
¼ teaspoon (1 ml) ground cloves

1 2
3 4

1	Preheat the oven to 400°F (200°C). Put the vegetables and herbs in a baking dish and drizzle with the oil. Sprinkle with salt.	2	Roast for 50 minutes, until the tomatoes are soft.	
3	Transfer to a blender and blitz until smooth, or use a handheld blender.	4	Strain the puree through a sieve to remove the tomato seeds and skins.	➤

| 7 | Put the tomato puree in a pan, add the remaining ingredients and stir over low heat until the brown sugar has dissolved. Bring to a boil and cook until the mixture is thick but still pourable. Season with salt and pepper to taste. | **TIP**
❋
Use ripe cooking tomatoes for this recipe — plum (Roma) tomatoes will give the best flavor. |

| 8 | Spoon the ketchup into dry, sterilized jars and label and date. Chill in the refrigerator after opening. | **NOTE**
❋
Once opened, use this ketchup within 6 weeks. |

PAPAYA CHUTNEY

❧ MAKES 6 JARS (1 CUP/250 ML EACH) • PREPARATION: 20 MINUTES • COOKING: 40 MINUTES ❧

2 pounds (1 kg) firm, slightly underripe papaya
10 ounces (300 g) onions (about 2 medium), chopped

2 green apples, peeled and chopped
3 tomatoes, chopped
1 cup (250 ml) packed brown sugar
1 cup (250 ml) balsamic vinegar

1 cup (250 ml) white wine vinegar
2 dried red chili peppers
4 slices fresh ginger

1 2
3 4

1	Cut the papaya in half, peel, remove the seeds and then roughly chop the flesh.	2	Put the papaya, onions, apples, tomatoes, brown sugar, vinegars, chilies and ginger into a pan and stir over low heat until the sugar dissolves.
3	Bring to a boil and cook for 30 minutes, until the chutney is thick and pulpy.	4	Spoon into dry, sterilized jars and seal with vinegar-proof lids. Label and date. Allow to rest, then chill after opening.

APPENDIXES

PECTIN, STORAGE & SEASONAL FRUIT & VEGETABLE CHARTS

INDEX

ACKNOWLEDGMENTS

PECTIN CHART

FRUIT	PECTIN	ACID
APPLES (COOKING)	high	high
APRICOTS	medium	low
BLACKBERRIES (EARLY)	medium	low
BLUEBERRIES	medium	high
CITRUS FRUIT	high	high
CURRANTS (RED, BLACK, SWEET, WHITE)	high	high
DAMSONS	high	high
FIGS	low	low
GOOSEBERRIES	high	high
PEACHES	low	low
PEARS	low	low
PLUMS	medium	medium
QUINCES	high	low
RASPBERRIES	medium	medium
RHUBARB	low	low
STRAWBERRIES	low	low

◆ Pectin is a gummy substance found in differing levels in fruits — it is the pectin in fruit that sets a jam.

◆ Pectin is mostly concentrated in the cores, skin, pith and seeds, and these are often used, usually wrapped in cheesecloth, when making jams with fruit that has a low pectin content.

◆ Slightly under-ripe fresh fruit contains more pectin than riper fruits.

◆ Cooking the fruit also helps to draw the pectin out of the fruit.

◆ You can also purchase special gelling sugar, which has pectin added to it and will take away any of the worries about whether your low-pectin fruit is going to set as a jam.

STORAGE CHART

STORAGE TIMES	
❖ THE CHART BELOW SHOWS THE KEEPING TIMES OF RECIPES IN THIS BOOK ❖	
Jams	Store for up to 1 year; refrigerate after opening and use within 1 year.
Marmalades	Store for up to 2 years; refrigerate after opening and use within 2 years.
Jellies	Allow 1–3 weeks for flavor to develop before eating. Keep for up to 1 year; refrigerate after opening.
Mustards	Allow 2–4 weeks for the flavor to develop before eating. Keep for up to 3 months; chill after opening.
Cheeses & butters	Use cheeses and butters within 1 year.
Curds	Store for up to 2 months in the refrigerator.
Chutneys & relishes	Store for up to 1 year; refrigerate after opening; use relishes within 6 weeks.

SEASONAL FRUIT & VEGETABLE CHART

→ This chart shows when a particular fruit is in season. ←

NOTE: For the southern hemisphere, reverse the months.

FRUIT	SPRING			SUMMER			FALL			WINTER		
	MARCH	APRIL	MAY	JUNE	JULY	AUG.	SEPT.	OCT.	NOV.	DEC.	JAN.	FEB.
APPLES							✳	✳	✳	✳	✳	✳
BEETS					✳	✳	✳	✳				
BLACKBERRIES					✳	✳	✳	✳				
BLACK CURRANTS					✳	✳						
BLUEBERRIES					✳	✳	✳					
CHERRIES				✳	✳	✳						
CHILI PEPPERS						✳	✳	✳				
CUCUMBERS					✳	✳	✳					
DAMSONS						✳	✳					
ELDERBERRIES						✳	✳	✳				
ELDERFLOWERS				✳	✳	✳						
FENNEL				✳	✳							
FIGS						✳						
GOOSEBERRIES				✳	✳							
LEMONS	✳								✳	✳	✳	✳
ORANGES											✳	✳
PEARS							✳	✳	✳			
PLUMS				✳	✳	✳	✳					
QUINCES							✳	✳	✳			
RASPBERRIES (SUMMER)					✳	✳	✳					
RASPBERRIES (AUTUMN)						✳	✳	✳				
RED CURRANTS					✳	✳						
RHUBARB	✳										✳	✳
RHUBARB (FORCED)		✳	✳	✳	✳							
STRAWBERRIES			✳	✳	✳	✳	✳					
SWEET PEPPERS				✳	✳	✳						
TOMATOES					✳	✳	✳					

✳ available and in season (lowest prices, lowest environmental impact)

INDEX

ACKNOWLEDGMENTS

I absolutely loved every minute of writing, testing, tasting and styling this delicious book, and, once again, I have the wonderful Catie Ziller to thank for offering it to me and for choosing such gorgeous colors. Thanks to Alice Chadwick, for adding all her special touches — your talent and humility are such a source of inspiration for me. My third arm, Kathy Steer, editor and so much more — organizer of crossing the t's and dotting the i's extraordinaire, bless, bless, bless. Clive Bozzard-Hill — my lovely photographer, for the beautiful images of the fizzing fruits and for being you.

The divine Kirsten Jenkins, the seedling that fed and watered herself and got to the place she dreamt she'd one day be. Welcome to the world of cookbooks. What a sensational job you did, and what an honor and joy to have you in the kitchen alongside me. Would you like a bag with that? The bush spice king, Scottie Foster, cheers, mate, for helping me test and taste all the recipes; your and the girl's input were crucial and much appreciated. Sarah Tildesley, my angelic "can't get enough lamps" beloved friend, work colleague and roommate. Thanks for making your home mine, lending me all the little bits that helped make this book as stunning as it is and for showing me that when love happens there is nothing more beautiful on this earth.

Dave Boyce, super surfer, Mr. Fix-It, Pridey's adoptive daddy, you are a legend, and I am forever grateful to you for the love and exercise you give my girl when I can't be here. Annie Mac, my darling saintly friend for helping me keep my business ticking while I am overseas; thanks so much for being so efficient and just being the amazing you I simply adore. And finally to all those people who purchased the jams and chutneys, providing me with funds to help my rebuilt Tibetan family's business, thank you for your generosity.

Life is definitely better with jam, chutney, fruit butters and jellies — I can vouch for it. I have eaten more than a whole nation would in a year in the last six months. And I still want more!